1

Barbara Zimmer 9/21/1984

the price

the price

the true story of a Mormon who defied Hitler

Karl-Heinz Schnibbe

**With
Alan F. Keele
Douglas F. Tobler**

Bookcraft
Salt Lake City, Utah

Library of Congress Catalog Card Number: 84-71070
ISBN 0-88494-534-0

First Printing, 1984

Lithographed in the United States of America
PUBLISHERS PRESS
Salt Lake City, Utah

To Helmuth

Contents

Preface

While I played a part in the drama, Helmuth Huebener is the hero of this book.

If you should go to Berlin, you probably will visit the National Memorial to the Victims of Fascism at Ploetzensee, an infamous old Nazi prison and execution site. There you will begin to understand what was happening in 1945, at the end of World War II, as the enormity of the Nazis' crimes against humanity was being fully revealed. There you will comprehend in a measure how significant is the memory of the courageous German martyrs who resisted the evil regime. Helmuth Huebener was the youngest of those martyrs. He was seventeen when he paid the ultimate price.

Helmuth has become one of the best-known members of the German Resistance. Hundreds of books and articles—in both Germanies—contain references to the Huebener Group, and Helmuth is a frequent character in major postwar German literary works. In our home town of Hamburg, a plaque adorns the place where he worked. Streets and public buildings, including the Helmuth Huebener Haus—an important educational, vocational, and recreational facility for young people—bear his name. Anniversaries of his birth and death are regularly celebrated by representatives of major political, civic, and church groups. For modern Germans, then, he is an example to be admired by young and old.

From personal knowledge of him I believe he deserves that admiration. Helmuth, Rudi Wobbe, and I grew up together as teenage friends in Nazi Germany. We could not know then that the course of our lives would bring us to non-violent resistance to Hitler which would eventually cost

Helmuth his life, and Rudi three and a half years and me seven in prison camps at hard labor.

While Helmuth Huebener's story is well known in Germany, many English-speaking Latter-day Saints know little or nothing about his life and death. Since my story is so closely related to Helmuth's, I hope reading this book will bring them that information as well as the inspiration of his willingness to pay the price.

The Nazis Take Over

On the day my world caved in I was with another painter decorating an empty apartment in Hamburg. A knock came on the door. I opened it to find two men standing there in long leather coats and soft-brimmed hats. One held a badge in his hand.

"*Geheime Staatspolizei. Bist du Karl-Heinz Schnibbe?*"

"*Ja.*"

"*Mitkommen!*"

I have no difficulty in remembering that it was noon on Tuesday, February 10, 1942.

The Gestapo (Secret State Police) took me to the prison at Fuhlsbuettel, where SS guards, members of Hitler's elite security police, kicked me, beat me, and threw me into a cell. All night long I lay wide awake, knowing that at any moment a guard might again turn on the harsh, bright lights, slam open the door of my cell, and perhaps beat me again with his heavy keys on their large iron ring.

My mind raced, flooded with thoughts of people, events, and decisions which might have brought me to this place. I had tried to conduct myself as a good member of German society and a faithful Latter-day Saint—and now here I was in the hands of the feared Gestapo, a youth of only eighteen years of age but in danger of being brutalized or even killed. How had it happened?

Years before I was born, even before my father had met my mother, one of the first links in the chain had been forged: my father had joined The Church of Jesus Christ of Latter-day Saints.

My father, Johann Schnibbe, was a farm boy from Hetthorn, a beautiful place in the North German moor country. Late one winter night his father left a tavern on his bicycle, tumbled into a ditch full of icy water, and caught a fatal case of pneumonia. He died soon after this.

The farm could not support the three sons he left behind, so in 1911 my father went to Hamburg, where he joined the merchant marine. Later he worked for the Woermann Lines as a stevedore. It was here that the all-important event occurred: he met Karl Verhahn, a fellow stevedore at the port—and a Latter-day Saint.

Dad was immediately interested in what Verhahn had to say about the gospel. He even followed him to a dingy meetingplace in an old school, where he spoke with the five or six other "Mormons." From that moment, he knew there was something to this church. He studied, read books, asked questions, and in 1919 was baptized a member. Thereafter he was an enthusiastic and totally converted Latter-day Saint, proclaiming the gospel to any or all who would listen to him, and to some who would not.

When my mother met him in 1920 she told him he was "nuts," but he persisted and eventually converted her, too. She was also from a modest background. Her father, Fritz

Luetkemueller, was a cabinetmaker from Luedelsen, a place about 150 miles southeast of Hamburg. He too had come to Hamburg as a young man. He lived with us in Hamburg after his wife died, and I remember that he drank a lot, too, just like my grandfather Schnibbe.

The Church of Jesus Christ of Latter-day Saints was the agent which pulled both my father and my mother, and through them me and my brother and sister, away from usual national and familial traditions and pointed us all in a new direction—a direction which would have a most profound influence on my life.

Times were generally hard in 1921, when my parents married. Inflation ran wild. In 1914, before World War I, one U.S. dollar had been equivalent to just over four German marks. In 1919, a dollar was worth almost nine marks; by 1921, the ratio was 1:77. In early 1923, it was 1:18,000 —and by November of 1923, it was 1:4,200,000,000,000! By then even a book of matches cost millions, billions, or even trillions of marks. Workers were paid every day, and they spent the money immediately, for the next day it would be worth even less. Food was scarce, and it was difficult to buy enough coal to keep apartments heated to drive out the damp, north German cold. During this difficult postwar period, many people died of malnutrition, pneumonia, tuberculosis, and other related diseases. Sometimes my father had a shortened work week, but all during the inflation of the early twenties and the depression of the thirties he managed to work fairly steadily.

Later on, although the Nazis blamed these difficult times on the Weimar Republic, my parents did not. Like Grandpa Luetkemueller and most families in our particular working-class neighborhood, they were supporters of the Republic and of the labor unions. Like most union members, my grandfather was a Social Democrat and he had a black, red, and gold flag that he hung out of the window on holidays. He also had a little insignia for his lapel with three arrows and the word *freedom* on it. So it was clear to all that he was a supporter of the Republic.

My father was not an actual member of the Social Democratic Party, but he was sympathetic to their goals. In fact, even though he looked back at the Empire as a time of stability, I remember my father referring to the Kaiser as a "pompous jackass." But my parents and grandparents were certainly not Communists, either. Very few people in our Hohenfelde neighborhood were. There were more Communists living further down in the city, in Barmbek, Altona, or Rothenburgsort. And further down by the Alster Lake there were some upper-class families. But our area was distinctly working class and we were always conscious and proud of it.

My father, like most German fathers of the time, was quite strict; my brother and sister and I were physically punished when we did something wrong. Because my parents were strict, I worked relatively hard at school; that is, I did my homework, although I was not a really serious student. I knew that I could never go to the university; most people from our class could not afford it. As far as my parents were concerned, education was vocational training. As soon as I was old enough I was to begin learning a trade.

At first I talked about becoming a sailor, but my father, who had been a seaman himself and was acquainted with the sometimes unsavory elements of that way of life, said that I should first get a vocational skill. So I went to school. I was the only Latter-day Saint in my school, but that did not affect my relations with the other students. We played together happily—religious differences didn't affect us.

The German schools of that time taught no civics or government, though in retrospect I can see that we were sorely lacking in knowledge of that subject when it came

The Schnibbe family in 1932 on balcony of the family apartment. Front, left to right, Berthold, Karla, and Karl-Heinz, age eight.

time to vote for or against the Nazis. Some, in fact many, of our teachers were Social Democrats, but there was no attempt made at school to teach us about politics. It has been said that we lived in a republic without republicans and a democracy without democrats. Later, when the Nazis came to power, everyone was indoctrinated in their particular version of political reality.

Most of the older Social Democratic teachers were forced to retire or join the party, and their younger replacements were often Nazis. I remember Herr Rolf,[1] an enthusiastic Nazi teacher I had sometime around 1936. Once, when I disagreed with him about some political issue, he said to me, "Schnibbe, you'll land in jail yet." Some of the other students laughed. Yet he was right.

Like any good German *Hausfrau*, Mother went shopping every day. She didn't have a refrigerator, of course—just a little pantry with a small open window covered by a grate, so that things stayed cool. Her daily round included stops at the milk store, the grocery store, the butcher shop, and the fruit and vegetable shop. Once a week there was a fish market and once a week a farmer's market. We always liked to go there because the vendors gave out free samples to nibble on.

And we had a fairly large garden, about an hour's walk from home, in the Dunckersweg, in Horn, near a well-known horse racing track. Our garden was not only a source of relaxation, recreation, and fresh air, but also vital to our family economy. We carefully cultivated and lovingly preserved all kinds of fruits and vegetables, rhubarb, black currants, red currants, gooseberries, peas, and beans.

With all the strenuous housework she had to do, it is no wonder that my mother did not have a job outside the

---

[1] Some names have been changed in this book.

home. Besides, it simply was not customary for women to work then. Women were expected to stay home and cook big meals every day, except on washdays, when Mom made our favorite dish: rice pudding with sugar, cinnamon, and milk.

One or two days a week we had fish. Since we lived near the port, fish was relatively inexpensive and there was a good assortment, from green herring to red snapper to shellfish and flounder. On Sunday we often had meat— *Sauerbraten, Rouladen,* a roast of some kind—but it was very expensive. During the week we sometimes had cold cuts for supper, but Mom always fixed our open-face sandwiches for us, and that was all there was to eat. No more. We never went to bed hungry, but we probably could have eaten more. Real hunger was something I was yet to learn about firsthand.

The American LDS missionaries came often for meals. Every day they went to some Church member's home for dinner—it was simply taken for granted that the members would care for them. When his mission was over, the missionary usually had saved enough money to travel through Europe. But we didn't care. We loved the missionaries and looked up to them.

We young people were especially fascinated by them —by their Americanness, by their broken German, and by what seemed to us their vast wealth. Even though these missionaries were probably from very poor homes them- selves, they always talked as though they were very weal- thy. Every one of them had a car and a house, and to us that was wealthy. Consequently, it never entered my mind that I could go on a mission; I wasn't an American, and we weren't wealthy. I believe most other young German Latter-day Saints felt the same. And yet, there was something distinctly evangelical about our later resistance activities; like the LDS missionaries, we were attempting to inform people about the truth by handing out leaflets. Ours were, in essence, political tracts.

From the missionaries we knew that America was Zion, the promised land, the land of unlimited possibilities. Yet there was no talk of emigrating to America; we were all very patriotic. We loved our beautiful north German city, from which large ocean liners of the Hamburg-America line departed for exotic ports of call, along with our large merchant marine fleet. Ironically, it was this surge of national pride out of which Hitler was making, and was yet to make, such great political capital all over Germany.

Perhaps the Latter-day Saints in a port city like Hamburg felt that they had, in fact, already been gathered to Zion out of the very worldly community in which we lived. For example, we were all very strong, almost fanatical, about the Word of Wisdom, even though there were bars on every street corner. We were simply in the world but not of the world.

My father was very much caught up in the Word of Wisdom. He used to preach temperance to my grandfather Luetkemueller, but finally had to give up. Nevertheless, he was always the preacher—when he gave a talk someone invariably had to tug on his coattail to tell him his time was up. He studied a great deal in the holy scriptures and in the few Church books available to us; consequently, he acquired quite a great deal of knowledge about the gospel. He became a travelling elder in the district—the one who took the sacrament to shut-ins and others who could not come to church. He taught them and saw to their well-being. The Church was really his life, and it became my mother's, too. My parents' best friends—the Knapps, the Bergmanns, the Berndts— were all Latter-day Saints.

We children, of course, were a little less committed. On a warm Sunday we often wanted to go swimming, but were told, "Nothing doing. Your place is in church." When it came to fasting, Dad was a bit more lenient. "Well, you don't have to fast if you don't want to," he would say, "but since we're not cooking anything there'll be nothing to eat today. But you don't have to fast if you don't want to."

I don't mean that we didn't like church: we did, and all our branch experiences were very positive. We were a close-knit group and we had fun together. Even differences in social class were largely ignored; the Breis, for example, who were quite well off, were also our friends in the branch. There were Christmas parties with Santa Claus, and New Year's parties, and picnics at our garden, and sack races and remodelling parties at the branch house where President Arnold Soellner had arranged for refreshments. All these things remain as happy memories.

It was also in the branch that I became friends with Helmuth Huebener and Rudi Wobbe. Little did we know at the time that these friendships would become matters of life and death and would later be tested by persecution and torture.

As a youth I noticed the transition to Nazism somewhat gradually. I first saw the differences in our branch. Brother Peter Lapin and his boys joined the SA—the Nazi storm troopers known as Brownshirts—and they began wearing their uniforms to church. I don't think they were the brutal, streetfighter type; as I recall, they were musicians, and they belonged to a military band. The SA gave them something to identify with. Still, no one spoke about this or about any other political matter in the branch until later.

I think most people were cautious, adopting a wait-and-see attitude. And at first it was difficult to be critical of the Nazis, even for those who intuitively didn't like them, for they improved the economy and gave Germany a new sense of purpose and destiny. Even our family benefited somewhat, because my father had fewer short workweeks after the Nazis came to power. Of course, for those who had been

The St. Georg Branch, about 1936. Front row: fourth from left, Rudi Wobbe; fifth from left, Karl-Heinz Schnibbe. Second row: seventh from right, Otto Berndt, Senior.

unemployed for a long time, the improved economic climate was all the more welcome. In five years after the takeover, the unemployment rate dropped from above 30 percent to less than 3 percent.

I do not mean to overemphasize economic progress under the Nazis; actually, they really only helped other Nazis, and overall progress was very slow. The lowly worker remained the lowly worker, even under Hitler's vaunted National Socialist German Workers' Party. But when people are out of work and desperate, they grasp at any straw, even if the pay is low and the job has been created only by a rapid military buildup in the first place.

When Hitler came to power, on January 30, 1933, we were all herded into the auditorium at school to listen to his acceptance speech on the radio. All night, people paraded through the streets with burning torches, singing the *Horst Wessel* song and others:

> *Es zittern die morschen Knochen*
> *Der Welt vor dem grossen Krieg.*
> *Wir haben die Knechtschaft gebrochen,*
> *Fuer uns war's ein grosser Sieg.*
> *Wir werden weiter marschieren,*
> *Wenn alles in Scherben faellt,*
> *Denn heute gehoert uns Deutschland,*
> *Und morgen die ganze Welt.*

(The old rotten bones of the world
Are quaking about the great war.
We have broken the bonds of servitude;
For us it was a great victory.
We shall march on and on,
Even if all is destroyed;
For today Germany is ours,
And tomorrow the whole world will be.)

By and large, we children were excited by the Nazis. They were excellent propagandists. They came by with their brass bands and their flashy parades; we followed them, like the children following the Pied Piper, to their band concert, on some marketplace or park or meadow, and we listened to their oratory. We saw the exciting party congresses in the newsreels and we listened to other Nazi orators like Josef Goebbels on the radio. "The nation is getting back on its feet," we heard them say. There was new hope after years of political and economic decline. A kind of intoxication came over the entire population, especially the young.

Our neighbor, Otto Schulz, became a convert to Nazism and to the SA early on. He liked the excitement of brawling and felt that the party gave meaning to his life — yet he really was a nice man, basically, a very good man. In fact, after I was arrested he came very close to getting in trouble himself by trying to help me.

In 1936, when I was twelve, I joined the *Jungvolk*, the "Cub Scouts" of the Nazi party. Recruiters came through each neighborhood, carefully registering each boy. Scouting had been banned in 1934, so I never had a chance to become a Scout, even though I had looked forward to it and was a bit disappointed.

Still, all the children joined the *Jungvolk*, and at first it was very exciting. We went on overnight hikes, slept in tents, fought mock battles between our groups, and marched to the beat of parade-corps drums. We had campfires, of course, but also large bonfires on open places in the city to celebrate special pagan Germanic holidays such as the solstice festivals. And we sang all the sentimental patriotic songs, such as "Flamme empor, leuchte mit loderndem Scheine, ueberm Gebirge am Rheine." (Flame rise up, illumine with glowing light, above the mountains on the Rhine.) We had Nazi party *"Heimabende"* (home evenings) in a large warehouse right by the Kuhmuehlenteich (a pond near the Alster Lake), where we were indoctrinated about Hitler's life and thoughts, the beginning of the great movement, the failure of the first Nazi *coup d' état* or *Putsch* at the beer hall in Munich in November, 1923, Hitler's writing of *Mein Kampf* in Landsberg prison, and so forth.

But before 1933, whenever there was a Nazi rally, my grandfather always put his black, red, and gold Weimar flag on the windowsill right next to our neighbors' swastikas. To my knowledge, my parents never voted for the Nazi party or for the Communists—always for the Social Democrats.

After about 1930, when I wanted to go somewhere my parents would often say, "No, today you stay home; they're planning a big confrontation." They never really talked about politics, however; perhaps it was getting too dangerous already even to talk about. One day Dad came home and said, *"Schulz ist verschuett gegangen"* (Schulz has had it). In that way we learned that another of his colleagues at the port, who happened to be a Communist, had disappeared into a concentration camp.

Once Dad even contributed some money for the wives and children of some of these men, but the list fell into the hands of the Gestapo and the contributors were themselves arrested. Dad and Mom fasted and prayed about it and "sweat blood" for many weeks. Somehow the Nazis overlooked Dad's name, or perhaps they could not read it. At any event, he felt his prayers had once again been answered.

When I was fourteen I went into the Hitler Youth. It was much like the *Jungvolk*, except that we got to wear a dagger with the words *Blood and Honor* stamped on the blade. By this time, however, I was beginning to be disillusioned by the Nazis. My parents, especially my father, deserve a great deal of credit for this, because they always made subtle negative comments about the party.

When I needed a Hitler Youth uniform, for example—
the brown shirt with a shoulder belt and a neckerchief—Dad
said, "What for? If they want you in their party, let them buy
the uniform for you." When I told the Hitler Youth leaders
that we couldn't afford one, they gave me the uniform, but I
wore it very seldom. If someone asked, "Where's your
uniform?" I always replied, "In the wash." After I came home
from a meeting my dad often said, "Well, what kind of baloney did they teach you tonight?"

This parental attitude had a great deal to do with my de-
veloping scepticism, though I may not have been aware of it
at the time. I began to skip my Hitler Youth meetings as
much as I could. When the Hitler Youth leaders came to the
house to tell Dad about my truancy, he said, in mock indig-
nation, "Well, that's terrible! That has to stop! I'll give him
the thrashing of his life when he gets home! Thanks for telling me!" Later on he told me what he had said, and we both
laughed.

My father could see that Nazism, which relied on force
instead of freedom, enticing people to place their absolute
faith in a man and in a political system created by men, was
the diametrical opposite of the gospel of Jesus Christ; it was
to him a competing religious system. Hence he was sceptical
of Nazis from the beginning. In fact, soon after January 30,
1933, some of our neighbors had to warn him to "keep his
big mouth shut" because he had been openly critical of the
Nazis.

One day, when I had been expressly ordered to wear
my uniform but had once more gone to the Hitler Youth
meeting without it anyway, I was punished for *"Befehlsver-
weigerung"*—failure to obey orders. To a repeated *"Marsch,
marsch!"* I was forced to run around on a drill field, up
and down, back and forth. My tormentor was no older
than I was, so when I had had enough I went over to him

and told him to leave me alone. He yelled at me, so I punched him in the face. When I got home and told Dad about it, he just grinned.

"Now I don't know what will happen," I fretted.

"Well, what can happen?" he replied with a shrug. "Nothing."

I never returned to the Hitler Youth; soon thereafter I received a letter officially documenting my dismissal. Later on, when I was arrested by the Gestapo, it did not help my case that they had a file on me showing that I had been drummed out of the Hitler Youth for insubordination.

2

Helmuth Huebener

Despite my bad experiences in the Hitler Youth and my father's fine antifascist example, I doubt that I would have become an active member of a resistance movement if I had not known Helmuth Huebener. Not that I would have despised the Nazis less—but I may not have hit upon a particular plan of action like the one Helmuth had in mind. On the other hand, it may have been partially due to my intense dislike of the Nazis that Helmuth was himself moved further toward antifascism; I don't know. I think we influenced each other. I know that I told Helmuth about an experience I had in 1938 which left me totally shocked and horrified.

I was an apprentice by that time, painting and decorating homes in the rich sections of Hamburg, where many Jewish people lived. They were very kind to me, and I occasionally got into political discussions with them. I remember one Jewish lady in particular, Frau Doktor Frank, who told me that she thought the Jews were in no real danger. They were German citizens, after all, and some were veterans of World War I, and they were important people with friends in high places, and so forth.

But one day, on the way home from work, I saw some SS and SA officers loading a group of Jewish people onto a truck. They must have been some of the relatively few Orthodox Jews in Germany, for the men wore dark hats and coats and looked like rabbis. This was not long before the infamous "Crystal Night" in November, 1938, when synagogues were burned and Jewish places of business were vandalized (the broken glass on the streets gave the night its name). Here, too, a rather large crowd of curious citizens — perhaps a hundred or so — had gathered, some laughing and applauding the SS and SA.

I couldn't believe what I saw. I had heard that Jews were being mistreated, but this was the first time I actually realized what was happening. Even the old men and women and the little children were being pushed and kicked and spat upon and mocked by the troopers.

I watched for just a moment, and then, sickened, I ran weeping from the scene and went home and told my mother what I had witnessed. "Where were they taking them?" I asked.

"I don't know, either," Mom said.

"That's impossible! How can they do that?"

And Mother replied, "They can. If you're smart, just forget what you saw and leave it alone."

Not long afterwards, we began to notice that our family doctor, Dr. Caro, who also happened to be Jewish, was being boycotted by the government medical insurance office. Whenever we went there to get our medical insurance voucher and we told them our doctor was Dr. Caro, they began to give us funny looks and to say, "Don't you have any other doctor?"

And then Dr. Caro simply disappeared. One day he was in his office as usual—and the next day there was a sign on the door reading "Closed." That was all. He was the doctor who had delivered me into the world. He was a gentle, fine man, who didn't hesitate for a minute to come when people in the neighborhood needed him. He had been a dear friend to our family—and now he was gone. Frau Doktor Frank also disappeared shortly thereafter. I think she may have been able to get out of Germany in time and emigrate to the United States, but if so, she would have been among the last to escape.

I was by this time, as I said, an apprentice decorator and painter. At age fourteen, near the end of March, 1938, a few weeks before leaving school, I went down to the government career advisement bureau. "What do you want to be?" the counsellor asked me.

"Well, I wanted to be a sailor, but my dad thinks that's an immoral life and he wants me to learn a trade. Since I still like the sea and ships, I'd like to be a ship's plumber or a marine steamfitter or something like that."

The counsellor said, "Hmm. I don't think we have any openings in those areas right now. What else can you do? What's your favorite subject in school?"

"Art," I told him, and he sent me home to get some pictures that I'd drawn with colored pencils. When he saw them he said, "You don't want to be a plumber; you want to be an interior painter—a decorator."

When he said that, I was immediately excited by the idea. He gave me the name of a firm—"F. Georg Suse, Painting Contractors"—where I could apply to become an apprentice under the master painter, Johannes Ehlers.

Because it was evening by then, I went to see Mr. Ehlers at home. Mr. Ehlers was very brusque with me. That's the way masters treated their apprentices in those days, I found out. They even boxed their ears occasionally. He barked at me for a while, and then he looked at my drawings. When he saw them, he said, "April first, 7:30 A.M., at the shop."

"Don't you want to see my school grades?" I asked, holding them out to him.

"Not interested. That's fine. You be there." I had the job; I was a *Dekorationsmalerlehrling.*

Once a week, on Tuesdays, I went to the vocational school in the House of Youth in the Museumsstrasse in Altona, where I learned theories, such as how to make bids and calculate materials, how to figure perspective for lettering, and how paint is manufactured. On Thursdays I went to the Nagelsweg, where the painting and decorating guild had a big six-floor apartment house that was kept empty just for us to practice on. The instructor, Herr Baehre, would come in with a large chisel, make big gouges and scratches on the door with it, and say, "I want this door perfect, beautiful."

I didn't start working on doors right away, of course. Being an apprentice in Germany in those days meant learning a trade literally from the ground up. For the first four or five months my job was to clean out the shop and to make deliveries to the eight or so journeymen working on jobs all over the city. After quitting time I chopped firewood for the boss's wife and I ran errands for her, too, such as grocery shopping.

As an apprentice I worked fifty to fifty-five hours a week, and I remember very clearly that during the first year I was paid exactly four marks eighty pfennig a week. I gave my mom 4.20 for groceries and for my white painter's clothes and I kept sixty pfennig for pocket money. The second year my pay was increased to 7.20 a week, and the third year to 9.60. The journeymen, by comparison, made just a little over one mark per hour, or about fifty marks for a forty-eight-hour week.

I was an apprentice for three years, after which I took the very difficult practical and theoretical journeyman's examination. Less than a year later, in February of 1942, my friends Helmuth and Rudi and I were arrested by the Gestapo.

We were, as I've said, friends from the St. Georg Branch. Because the Church kept us involved, almost all of my friends were other Latter-day Saints. My really close friends, however, were Helmuth Huebener and then Rudi Wobbe. They're the ones who often came to my house; and they're the ones with whom I went swimming or to the movies.

Helmuth was, simply stated, the smartest one in the group. He had tremendous talent. He could grab a pencil and whip out caricatures of Churchill and Hitler that were absolutely brilliant. And he was a natural leader—he got along well with people and everyone liked him.

He lived with his grandmother Sudrow and her husband, both good Latter-day Saints, and he was their favorite, I believe. They were too poor to spoil him, but they doted on him. Helmuth had two half-brothers, Hans and Gerhard Kunkel, who were about seven and five years older, respectively. He lived at the Sudrows', first because his mother worked a lot and later because she was remarried to a zealous Nazi named Hugo Huebener, whom none of the boys could stand. Before Hugo legally adopted him, Helmuth's name had been Helmuth Guddat, his mother's maiden name, or Helmuth Kunkel, her first husband's name.

Because Helmuth was a year younger than I, and because he went to the *"Oberbau"* or advanced track at school, he began his vocational training about two years later than I did. Helmuth went into the Hamburg city social welfare department, into what was called the *"obere Verwaltungslaufbahn,"* the upper administrative track. He was more of a white-collar apprentice, so to speak. If he'd been from a family with status and money he'd have certainly gone to the university, for he had the intellectual capability. He was very widely read and he loved to discuss things with me and Rudi and with adult members of the Church, as well as with people at his place of employment.

A few of the adult members at church remember him as being a bit arrogant, but I think it was because they resented—as any adult German at the time would have—the idea of a young person asking them difficult questions and pointing out flaws in their logic. Especially in political matters, where our Church members tended to be a bit naive, Helmuth enjoyed engaging adults in discussions, and picking their arguments apart if they were wrong. He enjoyed showing off his intellectual and debating abilities. But his intention was never to embarrass people. He only wanted to make them more careful about what they said— to make them back up their opinions more rigorously with logic and evidence. In our Sunday School, priesthood and MIA classes, Helmuth was the one who knew the answers. He had studied the gospel and he knew it very well for a person of his age.

We talked about the Nazi party and about Communism and the revolution. We had noticed the great emphasis on things military, and Helmuth said very early on, "Where can all this militarism be taking us—this Army Day, Navy Day, Air Force Day business? It can only mean one thing: war is inevitable. And these Hitler Youth uniforms look just like the military ones. Obviously they're preparing us to be soldiers, too." Helmuth used to say, "These Nazis are not *Parteigenossen* (party participants); they are *Parteigeniesser* (party partakers)."

Rudi was younger than both of us. His mother was a widow. Theirs was a good LDS family, and I spent a lot of time at their home on Sundays between our meetings. Rudi became an apprentice *Schlosser,* a mechanic or machinist, someone who works with metals. He, too, was not particularly fond of the Hitler Youth. He was riding his bicycle one day when a Hitler Youth patrol tried to stop him because he didn't salute their flag. He just rammed into one of them, knocked him over, and pedaled away. Since they didn't know who he was, they never caught him.

I hated those stupid flag patrols, too. Whenever they came along, everyone had to stand at attention and raise his arm in salute. I always turned a corner or stood in an alley or an apartment entrance if I could, and a lot of other people did, too, for Hamburg never did go completely over to the Nazis. There were too many Communists and Social Democrats there; besides, the place was just too cosmopolitan and independent, since it was an ancient Hanseatic free city, with close ties to England. Being aware of these things, the Nazis made Karl Kaufmann the *Gauleiter* or district administrator there, since he was a sophisticated cosmopolitan himself, not a typical Nazi thug like some of the other *Gauleiters* around the *Reich.*

Naturally our increasingly sour attitude toward the Nazis and Helmuth's outspoken political discussions with Church members did not find favor with everyone. Some of the branch members came through as Nazi sympathizers. It was even suggested that we start our meetings with the Hitler salute and sing the national anthem. Also that someone bring a radio so that the branch members could listen to Hitler's Sunday radio broadcasts together, with the door locked so that no one could leave during the speech. All these things were opposed, however, by people like my dad and Otto Berndt, who was a counsellor in the branch presidency at the time and who would eventually be the district president. "Don't you start that," Berndt said in response to such suggestions. "This is a church of God, not a political meeting." For the most part his view prevailed, but some time before the war a sign went up on the meeting-house reading Jews Not Allowed to Enter.

Of course we all knew that the meetings were being monitored, and we felt that some displays of patriotism were good insurance, such as the posting on the bulletin board of letters to and from LDS soldiers serving in the military. Once I saw at the branch some Hitler Youth members whom I recognized from my own days with the Hitler Youth. I said to them, "Hey, what are you guys doing here? You're not interested in our Church!" They had come to make a disturbance, but they left quietly a little later. Perhaps they lost their courage, or perhaps they saw one of our leaders in his uniform. I don't know.

Even after the war started in 1939, and as late as 1941, I observed that many members of our branch supported the regime, albeit somewhat nervously. "Well, we are fighting against Communism," they would say, "and we have to support the powers that be, as the twelfth article of faith says. And besides, our boys are out there on the battlefield." But at the end of 1941, when the United States came into the war after Pearl Harbor, many of the German Saints began to predict the defeat of Germany because of the Book of Mormon prophecies concerning the fate of those "gentile nations" which fight against "Zion." And after Stalingrad and other major defeats, this pessimistic attitude among the Latter-day Saints became even more prevalent.

I do not wish to leave the impression that any of the

Saints were evil people. They were not. Caught up in the dilemmas of the day, they perhaps became confused on the issues, but basically they were good people. And we had a fine branch. Brother Soellner was a dedicated branch president, a natural leader of old and young alike, who made things happen. Under his leadership we enlarged the branch meetinghouse and installed a baptismal font, and he made sure there were always cake and hot chocolate for the volunteer workers. An executive in a laundry detergent factory, he had workers under him there, so he knew how to organize people and get things done.

We had an active choir, which met on Fridays, and some of us younger people sang in it. I enjoyed it very much. In addition, my father and I were assigned five or six member families to visit, and we did it every month without fail. Our families lived in widely scattered parts of town; since no one had a phone, we simply had to walk to their homes, hoping they'd be there. If they weren't, we'd come back later. If they were, my father would give them a long lesson, forty-five minutes to an hour each, and then, invariably, the family would ask me to close the meeting with a prayer. Frankly, I didn't exactly enjoy that last aspect of our Church activity!

Relief Society and priesthood meetings were on Mondays, Mutual Improvement Association was on Wednesdays. On Sunday morning from ten until twelve we had Sunday School; at seven in the evening, we held sacrament meeting.

It was during one of these sacrament meetings in the summer of 1941 that Helmuth leaned over and whispered to me, "Come to my house tonight; I want you to hear something. But wait until after nine, when my grandparents are in bed."

3

Recruits
for the Cause

When I arrived at Helmuth's grandparents' apartment in the Louisenweg, I found Helmuth hunched over a small radio, a beautiful little Rola which his brother Gerhard had brought back from occupied France. Helmuth had pried open the cabinet in which the radio had been locked away when his brother left for the front, and had rigged up an antenna for the radio and had plugged it in. Now we sat together in the darkened room with the dim light of the dial illuminating our faces, the volume turned way down and our ears next to the speaker. Through the wall in the next room his old grandfolks were snoring away. Then, at exactly 10:00 P.M., we heard the first four notes of Beethoven's Fifth Symphony, the famous V-for-Victory code that had become the trademark of the British Broadcasting Corporation. *"Die BBC London sendet Nachrichten in deutscher Sprache,"* the voice said. It was the daily German-language news report beamed at the Continent in shortwave. The Nazis often tried to jam such broadcasts, but on this night it was crystal clear.

Just a few weeks before, on June 22, 1941, the German armed forces had launched their invasion of the Soviet Union, an operation which Hitler had code-named "Barbarossa." The official German military press releases about Barbarossa printed in the papers and broadcast on German radio stations boasted of great successes in Russia. According to the *Reichssender Hamburg*, the number of enemy soldiers killed and captured was phenomenal, but little or no mention was ever made of German losses. However, the BBC shortwave newscast gave Allied and Axis casualty figures, and there were enormous discrepancies between the British and the German accounts. "That can't be," Helmuth whispered to me, "somebody's lying!" And then I remembered other recent discussions with Helmuth at the church. He had said, on several occasions, that the *Wehrmachtsbericht*, the military press releases, were lies.

"Do you believe them?" he asked us.

"Why not?" we replied. "Why shouldn't we believe them?"

"Because they're lying, that's why," Helmuth retorted.

I had also heard that his friends at work called him "the man with connections," and now I suddenly realized what his source of information was. He must have been listening to the BBC for several weeks. "Do you realize that the Germans have reported the sinking of the aircraft carrier *Ark Royal* three separate times?" Helmuth hissed. "I've been keeping track.

"Look," he continued, "it just doesn't make sense. We march into Russia and kill so-and-so many of their soldiers. But they have guns. They're shooting back! I mean, put two and two together and you'll see that we're going to have some casualties on our side, too! And these British reports have a lot more details than ours, and they give their own casualties, not just the enemy's. Our news reports sound like a lot of boasting—a lot of propaganda—and theirs sound more realistic. I'm convinced they're telling the truth and we're lying!"

The broadcast ended at 10:30; I slipped out of the house and went home. But when I saw Helmuth next, I said, "Hey, if you're listening again, can I come and listen some more?" He said, "Sure."

That's how it started.

But there were some problems. Although I was already seventeen, my parents were still quite strict with me and they wanted me home by nine-thirty. Yet they liked Helmuth and trusted him, and they probably trusted me more when they knew I was with him. Still, there were times when they wouldn't let me stay out that late—we often had air raid warnings and had to go into the shelters—or they were afraid I'd "wear out my welcome" with the Sudrows. Knowing that Helmuth had learned shorthand at the office and that he had already made some notes on the casualty figures, I ventured a suggestion: "Look, if there's something very interesting . . . why don't you take some notes on it so that I don't miss anything when I can't come?"

"Okay," he said.

This must have been near the end of July, 1941. Soon after this Helmuth surprised me with a small stack of handwritten leaflets. "Don't you think everybody in Hamburg is entitled to know the truth?" he said. "They don't all have a radio like this one."

"Well," I replied, not quite realizing what they were for, "what about them?"

"Telephone booths!" Helmuth said. "Mailboxes! Apartment houses! I've written on the leaflets, 'This is a chain letter, so please pass it on'!"

Last Part of "Leaflet P"—German Version

Soldaten der Arbeit! Soldaten an allen Fronten! Der Fuehrer hat Euch fuer 1942 die Entscheidung versprochen, und er wird kein Mittel scheuen, sein Versprechen diesmal zu halten. Zu Tausenden wird er Euch ins Feuer schicken, um das von ihm begonnene Verbrechen auch zu beenden. Zu Tausenden werden Eure Frauen und Kinder zu Witwen und Waisen gemacht. Ohne Erfolg! Die europaeische Front steht fest, und einmuetig ist der Ruetli-Schwur, auch ihr Versprechen, das Versprechen aller alliierten Voelker:

Wir wollen sein ein einig Volk von Bruedern,
In keiner Not uns trennen und Gefahr!
Wir wollen frei sein, wie die Vaeter waren,
Lieber den Tod—als in der Knechtschaft leben!
Wir wollen trauen auf den hoechsten Gott
Und uns nicht fuerchten vor der Macht der Menschen.

(Schiller, *Wilhelm Tell*)

Europaeisches Erwachen: Als Antwort auf die laecherlich-dreiste Behauptung der Achsenpropagandisten, dass die U.S.A. durch den japanischen Ueberfall schon in den ersten Monaten schwer mitgenommen wurde, und "Roosevelts Traum, auf dem europaeischen Kontinent ein Wort mitsprechen zu koennen, auch nichts weiter als ein Traum" sei, haben nun auf Nordirland amerikanische Luft-, Land- und Seestreitkraefte Stellung bezogen. Mag man in Berlin, Rom oder Tokio das gewaltige Ausmass dieser Landungsaktion verschleiern und mit spoettelnden Gesten ihre Glossen ziehen. Die Zeit wird es lehren, wer die Wahrheit sprach. Und dann, wenn die alliierten und amerikanischen Streitkraefte auf dem Kontinent Fuss fassen, amerikanische und britische Luftgeschwader Tod und Verderben ueber das Reich bringen, wenn die alliierte und U.S.A.-Flotte mit frischen Reserven wirkungsvoll in die Schlacht um den Atlantik eingreift, dann werden Taten eine beredte Sprache sprechen, dann wird man den illusionistischen Seifenblaesern aus der Berliner Wilhelmstrasse mit Hamlet nichts weiter entgegnen als:

"Worte, Worte, Worte!"

Last Part of "Leaflet P"—English Translation

Soldiers on the home front! Soldiers on all fronts! The Fuehrer has promised you that 1942 will be decisive and this time he will stop at nothing to keep his promise. He will send you by the thousands into the fires in order to finish the crime he started. By the thousands your wives and children will become widows and orphans. And for nothing! The European Front stands fast and the Ruetli-oath is unanimous, unanimous the promise—the promise of all Allied peoples:

> We want to be united now as brothers,
> Not separate in danger or in need!
> We wish to live in freedom like our fathers,
> Preferring death to living servitude!
> We place our highest trust in God Almighty,
> And fear no kind of wicked human power.
>
> (Schiller, *William Tell*)

The European Awakening has begun: In reply to the laughably audacious contention of the Axis propagandists that in a month or so the U.S. has already been badly damaged by the Japanese attack and that "Roosevelt's dream of having a say on the continent of Europe is nothing more than a dream," American air, land, and sea forces have now taken up positions in the north of Ireland. Berlin, Rome and Tokyo may try to veil the dimensions of this landing, and may gloss over it with sneering gestures, but time will tell who spoke the truth. And then, when the Allied and American forces set foot on the Continent, when American and British squadrons bring death and destruction over the Reich, when the Allied and U.S. fleet enters the battle of the Atlantic with fresh reserves, then deeds will speak an eloquent language; then with Hamlet, our only reply to the illusionary soap-bubble blowers in the Wilhelmstrasse will be:

"Words, words, words!"

The leaflets were very simple at first. There was some information from the BBC and a provocative statement such as "Do you know they are lying to you?" or "Hitler is a murderer," or "Don't believe the Nazi party." Later on they were to become more creative, containing original poems and imaginative essays. They were eventually disguised as official Nazi announcements with a swastika on the letter-head—and they grew in length and in the number of copies per leaflet.

Helmuth gave me six or seven of these first handwritten leaflets to distribute. I placed them in mailboxes and phone booths, and I even remember putting some into the pockets of coats hanging in the opera house. But I made sure that I never took any home, particularly after I foolishly showed one to Otto Schulz, our Nazi neighbor, and he said, "You stupid jerk, where did you get that? You burn that immediately, and don't ever bring one of those around here again! Do you want to get us all killed?" Thereafter, when I had any leaflets left over, I was always careful to burn them before I went home. This habit may have saved my family from even more problems, for when I was arrested the Gestapo searched our apartment very carefully.

At church on Sundays, Helmuth would sometimes say, "Hey, we haven't seen each other for a long time. Why don't you come over and visit me? Let's do something together!" That was our signal. Then I knew that Helmuth had written a new set of leaflets and wanted me to help distribute them.

At first, Helmuth had something for me about every two weeks. Then, as we got more and more caught up in the project, as Helmuth became more and more obsessed with the idea of disseminating the truth, and as our activity took on something like missionary zeal, he made a new pamphlet every week, and then twice a week. Altogether, in the eight or nine months that we distributed them, he must have writ-

ten about sixty different leaflets. He began using a typewriter, at first with carbon paper, and then in conjunction
with the branch duplicating machine.

Some of the titles were: Hitler Bears the Entire Guilt;
Hitler the Murderer; Down with Hitler; Who is Lying?;
They Are Not Telling You Everything; Where is Rudolf
Hess?; The Voice of Conscience; The Struggle Against the
Racially Inferior Bolshevists; The Nazi *Reichsmarschall*; I Have
Calculated For Everything; Victorious Advances in Glorious
Battles of Extermination; 1942—The Decisive Year; The
Fuehrer's Speech.

Because of his stenographic and typing skills, Helmuth
was a clerk to President Soellner, who needed someone to
type letters to the soldiers in the field and to do other
secretarial work. Soellner gave Helmuth a key to the branch
meetinghouse in the Besenbinderhof and Helmuth received
permission to take a typewriter—Soellner's own personal
portable at first, and later the branch Remington —and work
at home. Helmuth often said, "Our only real crime is taking
this paper from the branch."

One day in September or October of 1941, when I
went to Helmuth's, I was surprised to find Rudi Wobbe
there. Apparently he had been involved all along, but because Helmuth had been so careful, for several months neither of us had known about the involvement of the other.
Rudi was fifteen at the time, one year younger than Helmuth
and two years younger than I. Helmuth had recruited him
partly because he lived in Rothenburgsort, a Communist
neighborhood known for its anti-Nazi sentiment, where Helmuth wanted many leaflets distributed. "As long as you're
both here," Helmuth said, "I think we ought to agree on
what we'll do if we get caught. I'm sure they're head-hunting
for us by now. Anybody who gets caught takes the blame
for everybody. Okay?"

From left, Rudi Wobbe, Helmuth Huebener, Karl-Heinz Schnibbe. Taken about 1941.

"Okay!"

"Don't talk to anybody," Helmuth said. "It's too dangerous. Not to your parents, not to anybody! At church we'll just shake hands and say, 'How's it going? Everything okay?' 'Fine.' And that's all." I wish Helmuth had taken his own advice better.

Though he was certainly not reckless, Helmuth was actually the most confident, perhaps even the cockiest of the group, and I was the most cautious. But none of us had any illusions, really. We all knew about Buchenwald and the other *KZs*, concentration camps. People commonly said, "Watch out! You'd better shut up or you'll get sent to a *KZ!*" And after all, I'd already seen those Jewish people loaded onto a truck by the SS and SA, and I remembered very well the disappearance of Dr. Caro.

And then there was Heinrich Worbs. He was a Latter-day Saint from St. Georg who'd been sent to the concentration camp at Neuengamme for making a disparaging remark about a statue in honor of "another Nazi butcher." We knew he had been arrested, even when we started our campaign in the summer of 1941, but sometime in December of 1941 or January of 1942, he returned, a ruined man. He had signed an agreement not to talk about it, but since he knew he would die soon he told Otto Berndt all about it. Helmuth also talked with him about the camp. Worbs told them that he'd been kept in stocks with freezing water dripping on his hands. Then a guard would knock off the ice with a rubber hose "to keep your hands warm!" He showed his bruises to Otto, who was absolutely shocked by what he saw. Worbs died about six weeks after he was released from Neuengamme.

There was also the case of Brother Salomon Schwarz, a Latter-day Saint in Hamburg who looked Jewish and was generally held to be a Jew, even though he did not descend from known Jewish ancestors and had been raised a Protestant. It was partially to discourage his visits to the branch at St. Georg that the sign reading Jews Not Allowed to Enter went up. Salomon was welcomed at the Barmbek Branch. However, when he tried to get a certificate proving he was not Jewish, he was arrested by the Gestapo (for not wearing the yellow Star of David with the word *"Jude"* written on it in black) and placed in the ghetto in the Grindel area of Hamburg. He eventually disappeared. He probably died in the Theresienstadt concentration camp.

People with gallows humor were saying, *"Koepfe muessen rollen fuer den Sieg"* (Heads must roll for victory) in a wry takeoff on the railroad's propaganda slogan: *"Raeder muessen rollen fuer den Sieg"* (Wheels must roll for victory). After a law was passed in 1936 authorizing the death penalty for "enemies of the state," anything could get a person killed, and the death penalty was enforced so often in those days and for the smallest infractions that we witnessed filmed executions almost every time we saw a newsreel at the movies. Handbills all over the city announced more and more hangings and beheadings. Human life became a very cheap commodity in Nazi Germany. So it was no secret in Germany in 1941 that illegal listening, *Schwarzhoeren,* and antifascist propaganda activities were capital offenses. Even the BBC warned us about this, too, in a way. They reported about the camps and about the hangings and beheadings.

Every time I went to Helmuth's to listen I got butterflies in my stomach and then diarrhea. When I first distributed the leaflets I was very nervous and scared. I felt as though I had a package of TNT in my pocket. I moved very fast — zip, zip — and then disappeared. Later on I relaxed a bit, and then I actually began to enjoy it. Our activity was part game and part adventure, but it was mostly deadly serious. I had never been one to engage in pranks, and this was far more than a mere prank. We wanted people to know the truth.

We were not so naive as to think we could bring down the regime, but we hoped that with the chain letter idea, a "chain reaction" of discussion would begin and then more and more people would get angry or at least nervous and do something themselves to resist Hitler. When I spoke with Helmuth I suddenly realized that Nazism was not merely a lot of minor annoyances and isolated infringements upon certain peoples' rights, but a thoroughgoing system of murderous, lying evil. Helmuth had inspired me to fight against this evil, and I saw no reason why we couldn't inspire others to do the same, even though Hitler's star was still rising; Germany was still victorious in war.

We knew that the Nazis were not totally immune to world opinion and to public pressure from within Germany. We had all experienced the euthanasia campaign when the Nazis had begun to kill handicapped people. They had shown us films in school and had taken us on field trips to the hospitals, trying to convince us how humane this was. But we remembered that the outraged opposition of one Catholic bishop, Bishop Galen of Muenster, had been sufficient to make the Nazis cease euthanasia. We felt then, and I still feel, that the pen is mightier than the sword, and that public opinion can do wonders, even in a dictatorship, if the people have courage.

Because Helmuth felt so strongly about this, I've always suspected that he may have attempted—perhaps successfully—to engage others in our activity, just as he had Rudi and me. I know he invited some of the other youth from our branch to listen to the radio, but I don't think they ever went. Perhaps I'm wrong; if there had been others, they would no doubt have stepped forward by now to receive the recognition and financial benefits of having been a resistance fighter. But perhaps they had reasons not to step forward, or perhaps they were killed in the bombing raids or at the front. I simply don't know how many people Helmuth tried to recruit. I do know, however, that his attempts to recruit new workers to our cause was to be the fatal step that led to our undoing.

One person I do know about was Gerhard Duewer, an eighteen-year-old fellow apprentice of Helmuth's whom I first saw when we were taken to Berlin for trial in August of 1942. I have since learned that Helmuth recruited Duewer at the *Bieberhaus,* their place of employment, to take a few pamphlets and show them to friends. Duewer claimed at the trial that he had gone once to Helmuth's room to listen to the BBC, but that the broadcast had been jammed that night. Duewer was a fairly reliable ally, even if only involved with Helmuth for a short time and even though he proved not hard to break under interrogation.

However, when Helmuth approached Werner Kranz, yet another apprentice at the *Bieberhaus,* and attempted to persuade him to translate a handbill into French for distribution to French prisoners of war working in Hamburg, he was observed by Heinrich Mohns, a fellow employee who also happened to be the Nazi *"Betriebsobmann,"* the overseer of loyalty and patriotism in the office. When Huebener and Duewer were out of the room, Mohns questioned Kranz about them. Next Mohns called in Duewer, who foolishly happened to have a leaflet in his pocket. Mohns then contacted the Gestapo.

The next day, Thursday, February 5, 1942, Gestapo Commissioner Wangemann and Officer Muessener arrived at the *Bieberhaus* to question Helmuth and Gerhard, afterward searching their homes. Duewer, of course, had been forewarned by his previous encounter with Mohns, but he had not warned Helmuth, possibly under Mohns's instructions. At Duewer's home, therefore, the agents found nothing incriminating, but at Helmuth's they discovered the radio, a pile of assorted leaflets—among them at least twenty-nine different ones, for they listed them all carefully—some notebooks with manuscripts of handbills along with some shorthand notes, and the Remington typewriter with seven unfinished carbon copies of a leaflet still in place in the roller.

At 5:00 P.M. on that Thursday, February 5, Helmuth and Gerhard were formally arrested. On the same day, three more pamphlets were turned in to the party block leader by a Frau Bertha Floegel, a Herr Schwedlick, and a Herr Frehse. All three leaflets were found within one block of Helmuth's house in the Louisenweg. (Surprisingly, however, relatively few leaflets had found their way into Gestapo hands before this time.)

I have since read the transcripts of Helmuth's interrogations and I know that he signed the first of several confessions only after two days of torture. Even then he mentioned me and Rudi only in passing, describing us more as curious friends than as fellow conspirators. At the time, of course, I didn't even know that Helmuth had been arrested. I hadn't seen him much over the Christmas holidays, and only a few times in January. Three days after his arrest, on Sunday, February 8, 1942, I went to church as usual, not even thinking it strange that Helmuth wasn't there. Although he seldom missed church, I simply assumed he was ill. Then, at the conclusion of the evening sacrament meeting, President Soellner stood up and said, "Brothers and sisters, something very tragic has happened. Please stay for a few minutes after this meeting. I have a special announcement to make."

"Well," I thought, "somebody must have been excommunicated or something."

Karl-Heinz shortly before his arrest, age seventeen.

At the special meeting a few minutes later President Soellner announced: "A member of our branch, Helmuth Huebener, has been arrested by the Gestapo. I cannot give any details because my information is very sketchy—but I know that it is political. That's all." But that was not quite all. President Soellner was apparently angry. "How could he have done that with my typewriter!" he said. "I trusted him fully!"

I felt as though I'd been hit with a club. The blood left my head, and my heart felt like it was about to leap out of my chest. I had never been so scared. I was literally sick. I looked at Rudi and he looked at me, his face pale, but we couldn't speak.

"What?" some other members of the branch were saying around me. "Helmuth? That's impossible!" I didn't wait for Rudi to leave; I just wanted to go home. I expected to be arrested myself, but I fervently hoped that Helmuth would remember our pact—that whoever got caught would take all the blame.

In my childhood I had become very interested and involved in amateur theatricals, and what little acting ability I had developed then I fully needed now, for I didn't want my parents to think anything was wrong. I couldn't tell them anything. But fortunately, they didn't talk about it much. People had become close-mouthed during the Nazi years. If anyone talked too much about anything, someone else might think he knew something. All my parents said was, "I wonder what he did."

4

Guests of the Gestapo

All through Sunday night, Monday, Monday night, I was afraid they'd come for me. But it didn't happen until Tuesday, February 10, right at noon. I was working in an empty apartment with a fellow journeyman painter and paperhanger named Willi Vorbeck—and there was a knock.

"I'll get it," I said, with a certain intuitive foreboding, and there they were: Officers Wangemann and Muessener, as it turned out, in their leather overcoats and their soft-brimmed hats. One flipped open his badge: *"Geheime Staatspolizei. Bist du Karl-Heinz Schnibbe?"*

"Ja."

"Weisst du, warum wir hier sind?"

"Jawohl."

"Mitkommen!"

I think I said yes to their question whether I knew why they were there because they looked so mean. I felt that I should be agreeable if I wanted to avoid a beating.

"Can I change clothes?" I asked.

"Nein."

"What's going on?" Willi asked.

"Never mind!"

"Don't worry about it, Willi," I said blithely. "See you later."

We went downstairs and got into the back seat of a Mercedes waiting at the curb. Wangemann sat on one side and Muessener on the other, with me in the middle.

"Where do you live?" the driver asked.

"Rossausweg 32."

"Where's that?"

"Hohenfelde."

"Oh, *ja.*"

When we arrived at my house, no one was home. Mom had gone to the dentist, Dad was working, and the others were away on various errands. I let us in with my key. "Just stay put," they said. Then they began to search.

"What's this?"

"That's our bookcase."

They grabbed the books and looked in them one by one, and then they looked behind it.

"Where's your bed?"

"Right there." And they looked under the mattress.

This lasted for about an hour. Naturally they didn't find anything, since I had never kept any leaflets at home. Eventually I was put back into the car. <u>Now the evil spirit I had felt from the minute they showed their badges got stronger until I felt it would destroy me.</u> The spirit I felt was unbelievable. These were evil men, on an evil mission. They drove me to Kolafu, which is an abbreviation for the words *Konzentrationslager Fuhlsbuettel*—the Fuhlsbuettel concentration camp. This was the Gestapo prison for political prisoners, but it was operated, like the other *KZs*, by the SS. Actually,

Karl-Heinz visiting the Gestapo prison at Fuhlsbuettel in 1984. This is now a memorial museum.

it was just one wing of a normal prison, the biggest prison in Hamburg.

A large gate opened, we drove in, and the gate closed behind us. I got out of the car and was led into a kind of administration building. There I was asked my name, and then I was told to stand against a wall. I walked over toward it when—pow!—I got a hard kick in the behind and someone screamed, "Run!" Then I reached the wall and stood facing them. Pow!—another kick. I had no idea of the procedures there, but I learned fast. Each prisoner had to run everywhere and always face the wall, with his nose almost touching it.

Within a few minutes they had taken me to a cell. One other prisoner was in there; I recall that he was Dutch. He said he'd refused to work for the Germans. He had been there for ten days or so, and they had beaten him badly. He looked very sick. After a couple of hours, one of those smartly uniformed SS men came in with his nightstick and his Lueger pistol hanging from his belt and a large key ring in his hand. The minute the door opened the Dutchman jumped up, leaped to the back of the cell, and cried "*Schutzhaftgefangener* So-and-so." I was supposed to do the same, I learned by means of a savage kick. "*Schutzhaftgefangener* Schnibbe," I cried out from then on. "Prisoner Schnibbe, in protective custody!" *Protective for whom?* I always wondered.

"Why are you here?" the SS man demanded.

"I don't know."

Pow!—the key ring hit me in the face. "Do you know now?"

"No, sir, I mean, yes, sir!"

"Why didn't you say so?"

I was sure that the cell was bugged and that they were trying to get me to confess right then and there. After two or three beatings, I finally said, "I allegedly listened to an enemy broadcast."

Pow!—"What do you mean, 'allegedly'? Did you or didn't you? You know, we've got your friend. And he sang plenty."

Then he left me alone for a while. But about every twenty minutes or so, the door would fly open and an SS man would saunter in, lift the toilet lid with his key ring, look around, and then leave. It was a kind of psychological torture.

Now that I was finally locked up and left alone for a time with the light out, a great weariness came over me. My nerves, which had stretched until I thought they would snap, began to relax a bit and to calm down. The darkness was comforting, somehow. I thought of home and of my parents, especially my mother. *They must be terribly worried about me*, I thought. Then the entire miserable situation hit me and I cried quietly into my pillow for a long time.

I had no idea what time it was when I finally stopped crying. I was weary in both body and soul, but I couldn't sleep. A thousand thoughts and worries flashed through my mind and kept me awake. I wondered how much anxiety and suffering this little cell had seen. My eyes were burning with fatigue, but still I couldn't sleep. Suddenly the door was slammed open again, the bright lights hit us brutally in the eyes, and we had to get up and run to the wall and tell the guard our names.

"I do hope I didn't wake you," the SS officer sneered at us. Then the door slammed again and it was dark. *What sadists!* I thought. *How could anyone with a soul and a heart do these things?* Little did I know that I would have to endure such treatment for seven years.

Early in the morning, and almost every day for about

three weeks, I was taken from my cell, placed aboard a police van—*die gruene Minna* (the green lady) as we called it—and taken, chained to a group of other prisoners, into town to Gestapo headquarters on the third floor of the main police station in the Kaiser Wilhelmstrasse. The *paternoster*, a kind of slow-moving elevator without doors which you just stepped onto after saying your prayers, was boarded up at the third floor and there was an SS guard at the big barricade near the stairs on that floor. It was a world with its own rules.

It was here that I saw Helmuth again, in a large room that we prisoners referred to as "the hall of mirrors" because it was so long. Painted a brilliant, glossy white, the room was brightly illuminated. About sixty men had to stand there with their noses to the wall until they were called in for questioning. As I entered the hall of mirrors, I saw Helmuth. He just happened to be near the door, in the only place I could have seen him at all, and he gave me a kind of grin, which I caught out of the corner of my eye as I went in. So I knew that he hadn't talked, and I decided to admit to as little as possible. But I could also see that he'd been beaten. His face looked very puffy and bruised.

Standing in this white room for hours on end, we often lost our equilibrium and fell over. As soon as someone did, a sadistic SS man would kick him up again. When this happened to me, they said, "So, you wanted to bring Germany to the fall—and now you're the one who's falling, right?" I learned to close my eyes a little bit and concentrate and then I could stand up. And I prayed. I prayed every ten minutes, at least. "Heavenly Father, help me out of this mess! Help me have the strength to endure!"

About a week after my arrest, I saw Rudi in the hall of mirrors, and I assume Duewer was there all along, but I had never seen him and didn't even know about him until later. I couldn't really turn my head to nod at Rudi or Helmuth, lest an SS man throw one of their heavy glass ashtrays at me, which was their method of enforcing their rules.

Eventually I was taken for interrogation into a smaller room with Wangemann, Muessener, and a stenographer. "I tried to listen once," I lied, "but it wasn't clear and I couldn't hear anything." Pow! "Didn't get a clear reception." Pow! But I stuck to my story, despite the punches and the kicks.

During one of these interrogation sessions they asked me something different. "Did you steal some bicycle tires from the attic of the house where you were working when you were arrested?"

"No."

"We didn't think so, but it was blamed on you."

As I thought about it—and I had plenty of time to think about it—I decided it must have been good old Willi Vorbeck, the journeyman I was working with when I was arrested. I had provided him with a perfect cover-up and he was not slow to take advantage of it.

Surprisingly, this question came as a refreshing change, for most of their questions were designed to find out who was behind our group. The Gestapo simply could not believe that a teenager had masterminded what we had done. In their minds, there must have been an adult who had put us up to it—and they were not easily persuaded otherwise. They had all the time in the world. They could send me back to the hall of mirrors for a while, or question me again the next day. They had other fish to fry in the meantime. I was the one who had no time; I was the one who wanted it over with. Sometimes when I sat in the cell at Kolafu for two days without being taken to the hall of mirrors and interrogated, I felt worse than when I had been with Wangemann and Muessener in the Kaiser Wilhelmstrasse.

Meanwhile, my parents were frantic. They had gone to the police and had been told nothing. For several weeks they did not know I had been arrested. Finally, around the end of February, 1942, I was transferred to the *Untersuchungsgefangnis* (investigative prison) on the Glockengiesserwall at the Alsterglacis. Here I was treated somewhat better. I was not beaten and I was not interrogated, though we were submitted to some psychological terror, for our cells were right above death row. There were between five and fifteen executions per day. Usually they picked up the first condemned man around 4:30 in the morning to take him to the guillotine. Some went calmly; some went screaming. It was awful.

After I was moved there, my parents were finally informed of my arrest and allowed to visit me. I was taken from my cell, placed in handcuffs, and led into the basement, where a tunnel connected the prison to the Justice Building. There, in an office, with a guard handcuffed to me, I saw my mother for all of five minutes. My father, she informed me, had been drafted into a job in a munitions plant out in the forest and he was not able to come. Mom couldn't say much more; she was heartbroken to see me in handcuffs, thin and pale. She just held me and sobbed. She was allowed to visit for five minutes once every four weeks.

I had no idea, as I waited there in my cell for almost six months, what was going to happen to me. I was not told anything. I had my dark blue prison uniform with the funny little round hat; I had only the toilet paper—little squares of old newspaper—for reading material; and I kept my cell spotless. That's all. I was not cold, because spring arrived, and then summer. I marched back and forth to keep my strength up: five steps one way and five steps back. Once they brought in another prisoner, a habitual criminal, but mostly I was in solitary confinement.

Every day I got a big glob of potato soup, which I ate from my *Buett,* an enameled bowl which resembled a small chamber pot. I had not been able to eat much in Kolafu, but now I ate whatever they gave me and tried to keep up my strength. In my cell there was one window, about twelve feet up, and I had a bunk, a toilet, a little chair, and a table. I was not allowed to sit on the bunk during the day, although when they turned the lights off at night I was allowed to lie down. I had nothing to write with. I was very lonely.

Around the first of August, 1942, after I had been in prison about six months, a man came in with the formal complaint—the *Anklageschrift*—and told me to read it; he'd be back for it in two hours. I opened it up. Though I had been troubled with constipation most of the time in prison, due to lack of exercise and to the poor diet, within seconds I had a bad case of diarrhea. The document had "Top Secret!" stamped all over it. *"Vorbereitung zum Hochverrat"* (conspiracy to commit high treason) and *"landesverraeterische Feindbeguenstigung"* (treasonous aiding and abetting of the enemy), the charges ran. And then I read that we were to be tried before the *Volksgerichtshof,* the feared blood-court in Berlin, Nazi Germany's highest tribunal. When I saw that I thought, *Oh man, we are all dead ducks!*

Not long thereafter we were transported to Berlin. The four of us—Helmuth, Rudi, Duewer, and I—were handcuffed, and then each of us was chained to his own individual guard like a common murderer. We were placed in a *gruene Minna* van and driven to the Altona train station, where we boarded an express train for Berlin. We had our own compartment, the windows of which were posted over with signs reading "Police Transport—Entry Forbidden!" How the people gawked at us! We prisoners sat together on one side, and the guards sat on the other. We could have talked if we had wanted, but we were all very quiet, even after the guards locked the door and removed our handcuffs.

When someone tried to look in, the guards pulled down the blinds.

Late in the afternoon we arrived in Berlin. A *gruene Minna* took us to Alt-Moabit, the oldest and dingiest prison in Berlin. There we were to sit until Tuesday, August 11, 1942, when we would be taken to the Bellevuestrasse, to the *Volksgerichtshof*, for our trial.

As I have learned since, the *Volksgerichtshof* was not the only body sitting in judgment upon us. Ten days or so after Helmuth's arrest, by local leader action the word *Excommunicated* was written on Helmuth's membership record. There is no evidence that a Church court was officially convened to consider the matter.

Perhaps it was felt that our arrests posed a danger to the Church that required the action taken, and maybe that was so. But I confess that that seemed unlikely to me as an exclusive motivation in view of the feelings I had seen exhibited favorable to Nazism.

For all that, I realize that by any stretch of imagination it must have been a tense time for the branch, and I certainly wish to extend to inexperienced local Church leaders working under such extreme circumstances all possible benefits of any doubt. We were the ones, after all, who had placed the other members in peril. If they can forgive us, we certainly can forgive them.

After the war, Otto Berndt (who had had no part in the negative action) made sure that Helmuth's "excommunication" was corrected. He and the new mission president, Max Zimmer, wrote "excommunication done by mistake" on Helmuth's membership record, dated it November 11, 1946, and signed it. Later, Max Zimmer's successor, Jean Wunderlich, notified the Brethren in Salt Lake of the affair, and a similar notation was placed on the Church's copy of Helmuth's record. One injustice, at least, had been corrected.

5

Trial and Sentence

At Alt-Moabit prison, we were again placed in solitary confinement and subjected to all kinds of verbal abuse. Prison officers called us *Schweinehunde, Lumpen, Verbrecher, Landesverraeter* (swine, scum, criminals, traitors), and it became clear once again that we had already been found guilty even before our trial.

During the week or so that we were at Alt-Moabit, we were each assigned a defense attorney; mine was Dr. Wilhelm Kunz. Here, too, it was evident that only the superficial formalities of what had once been a system of justice had survived Nazi rule: Dr. Kunz could not possibly really try to defend me. If he had said anything in my defense he'd have been arrested himself at once. He told me that he'd try to point out how young I was and he told me not to worry too much—that it wouldn't be so bad. I didn't trust him at all, and I didn't tell him anything of any importance. I stuck to my story. I was afraid he was really only an informer.

Finally the day came: Tuesday, August 11, 1942. Early in the morning we were handcuffed and loaded into a *gruene Minna* and taken to the Bellevuestrasse to the *Volksgerichtshof*. At about 8:00 A.M. the trial got under way. On the high bench at the front sat the judges, among them the vice president of the *Volksgerichtshof* Engert, *Oberlandesgerichtsrat* (chief justice) Fikeis, *NSKK Brigadeleiter* (motorized SA brigade leader) Heinsius, *Oberbereichsleiter* (superior district leader) Bodinus, *Oberfuehrer Gaugerichtsvorsitzender* (superior district judicial president) Hartmann, representing the Attorney-General of the Reich, *Erster Staatsanwalt* (first prosecuting district attorney) Dr. Drullmann, and *Justizsekretaer* (judicial minister) Woehlke. Next to Fikeis on the bench there were also a high army officer, a high SS officer, and a court stenographer. Fikeis and some of his associates were dressed in blood-red robes, each adorned with the bright gold eagle and swastika, an insignia cynics called the *Pleitegeier*, the "vulture of rack and ruin."

We, the accused, sat slightly elevated in the second row in front of the bench. Our attorneys sat below us and to the front; the press corps and the public sat behind. I was comforted to see my father there, the only person from any of our families who attended the trial. He'd come from Hamburg alone and was staying with friends who were members of our church.

The opening statements and all of the formalities lasted about an hour or an hour and a half. Then, for reasons of secrecy, the courtroom was cleared and the trial itself was closed to the public. Dad had to leave, as did the reporters and other observers. For about six more hours he waited outside while we endured a grueling rehearsal of every detail of our conspiracy.

Witnesses had been brought from Hamburg by the prosecution. The two Gestapo agents, Wangemann and

Muessener, were there, as was Werner Kranz, whom the court chided for not turning Helmuth in himself. A young soldier in uniform by the name of Horst Zumsande had been called to Berlin from his post in Thorn because Duewer had once shown him and his brother Kurt a leaflet. The main witness for the prosecution, however, was Heinrich Mohns, the office overseer of party loyalty. This man explained to the court that his job was to watch out for defeatist, "un-German" talk and to keep the office running in a most patriotic manner. (In 1949, for his role in the death of Helmuth Huebener, he would be placed on a list of war criminals and himself sentenced to prison.) The court spent only a little more time on Rudi, Gerhard, and me, then focused their full attention on Helmuth, clearly the leader.

To this day I'm amazed at how cool, how clear, and how smart Helmuth was. The court hashed over every detail in every leaflet. And he remembered everything: where and when he'd had an idea for a pamphlet, what he meant by this, why he'd written that. This had obviously not been a mere lark for Helmuth. It had been a work that he was deeply committed to.

All during the trial, Helmuth stood there like an oak and answered questions: "Why did you do what you did?" "Because I wanted people to know the truth." "Do you mean to tell us that British atrocity stories are the truth?" "Exactly!" His attorney, Dr. Hans Georg Knie, looked up at him as if to say, "Are you completely nuts?"

Occasionally Helmuth was even openly sarcastic with Fikeis. Fikeis continued to ask, "Do you mean to tell me that what the British are telling us is the truth? Do you believe that?" Finally Helmuth said, "Sure; don't you?"

It was clear to me then that Helmuth knew deep in his heart that he was doomed—that he'd been condemned to death even before he set foot in the courtroom. Therefore,

Helmuth Huebener shortly before his arrest, age sixteen.

he'd resolved to act with dignity and courage. When the court sentenced him to death, he said, "You kill me for no reason at all. I haven't committed any crime. All I've done is tell the truth. Now it's my turn—but your turn will come!"

By this time the spectators, including my father, had been allowed back into the courtroom for the sentencing. Fikeis continued to scream and yell at us, however, and call us names: vermin, scum, dirty Commies—by which he meant simply antifascists—who should all be exterminated. I was trembling all over, but Helmuth still stood there like an oak.

I was sentenced to five years at hard labor, Rudi to ten —no doubt because he had admitted too much and had talked too freely to an informant the Gestapo had put in his cell with him—and Gerhard to four because there was no proof that he had listened to the radio. And then the trial was over. It was 4:50 P.M.

We were handcuffed and led away into the basement. I'll never forget the line of people on either side of us who took off their hats and stood silently as we were dragged through the hallways and down the stairs. Everyone knew that the *Volksgerichtshof* almost always rendered the death sentence, but I'm sure it was a silent demonstration of support for us rather than mere morbid curiosity.

In the basement we were all locked in one room, still with our handcuffs on, and given a piece of bread to eat. I was still shaking like a leaf, but Helmuth quietly ate his bread. I finally recovered enough to talk.

"Helmuth," I said, "I don't think they'll do it. They'll commute your sentence or pardon you or something. They're just trying to make an example of you so that others don't do what we did. They won't kill you."

"Yes, they will," he replied calmly. "Look at the walls."

Then I noticed that the walls were completely covered

with scribblings. There was a name and then "Sentenced to death!" Another name and "Sentenced to death" followed. Other writings were there as well: "Why?" "I don't want to die!" "Good-bye, Louise, take care of the children!" It was awful. Helmuth knew too well that the *Volksgerichtshof* executed almost everyone tried there.

My father had written the court a letter pleading for clemency for me, and he had asked for permission to see me. The court was generous; they gave Dad two minutes. He came into the room, looked at me, and started crying. I put my arms around him and tried to comfort him. He was shocked at my sentence of five years at hard labor, though to me it was a great relief. Helmuth had been condemned to die, after all, and I'd expected that we'd all be executed.

Years later Dad asked me, "Do you remember what you told me that day?"

"No."

"You really gave me quite a pep talk. You said, 'Now come on, Dad, it's not the end of the world. I'm still alive. We all could have been sentenced to death.' "

But it was to hit me later on, after I'd said good-bye to Dad, and after I'd said good-bye—for the very last time—to Helmuth. When the guards came for us, we shook hands. I put my arms around him. Helmuth had very big eyes, and now they were filled with tears.

"Good-bye, my friend."

"Good-bye."

Then he was taken one way and we went the other. We were headed back to Hamburg, and he was bound for Ploetzensee prison there in Berlin—the place where he was to be executed.

No date had been formally set for his execution. For a prisoner to know that he could be taken out and killed at any time was simply part of the punishment. I have since learned that he was kept there in a maximum security cell, with no blankets or clothing allowed, lest he hang himself, from August 11 until October 27. Then, at twelve noon, Helmuth was informed that all appeals had been denied and that he was to be executed that evening.

During the next eight hours he wrote three letters: one to his grandparents, one to his mother, and one to the Sommerfeldt family, in whose home he had been more of a son than a friend. After he was compelled to drink some wine in order to dull his senses, something which greatly offended his LDS sensibilities, he was accompanied by a Lutheran pastor the few steps to the room containing the guillotine. His sentence was again formally read; the ancient custom of breaking the staff and pronouncing the phrase, *"Dein Leben ist verwirkt!"* "Your life is null and void!" was duly carried out; and at 8:15 P.M. the guillotine snuffed out his young life and his brilliant mind. His body was given to the anatomical institute at the University of Berlin for use as a cadaver. His grave is unknown.

Various groups, including the Hitler Youth in Hamburg, appealed Helmuth's sentence. Even the Gestapo were afraid it could cause an uprising among the workers there. But the *Reichskanzelei*, the Imperial Chancellery, the office of final appeal under Attorney-General Thierack, and Hitler himself turned them all down. After Helmuth's death, thousands of little red leaflets appeared all over Hamburg announcing the execution of this "traitor to his country." It was clear that the Nazis feared the truth more than they feared weapons, and leaflets more than guns.

Nine months later, in July of 1943, Helmuth's mother and grandparents were killed in a bombing raid on Hamburg. His farewell letters to them were destroyed. The one he'd written to the Sommerfeldts survived:

The room at Ploetzensee where Helmuth Huebener was executed. This Berlin prison is now a national memorial to the victims of Fascism.

Dear Sister Sommerfeldt and Family,

When you receive this letter I will be dead. But before my execution I have been granted one wish, to write three letters to my loved ones . . .

I am very thankful to my Heavenly Father that this agonizing life is coming to an end this evening. I could not stand it any longer anyway! My Father in Heaven knows that I have done nothing wrong. I am only sorry that in my last hour I have to break the Word of Wisdom. I know that God lives and He will be the proper judge of this matter.

Until our happy reunion in that better world I remain,

Your friend and brother in the Gospel,

Helmuth

On August 17, the Sunday after the trial, I was still in my cell at Alt-Moabit waiting to be transferred back to Hamburg. Only one hundred feet or so from the prison chapel, I suddenly heard the organ playing. Then I broke down completely and cried for hours. Much later, in 1949, after seven years of Nazi and Russian prison camps, I went with my mother into a church in Hamburg to listen to an organ concert. When the organ began to play, I again broke down completely and began to cry. People around us were concerned and rushed to my aid, but Mom just said, "Let him cry; let him wash it all out with his tears." I cried for over two hours. Even as I write this now I recognize for the first time the subconscious connection between the two events.

Back in my cell at Moabit I was smitten with guilt. *Helmuth has to die, and we get to live,* I thought. I wrote a letter to my parents apologizing for giving them so much trouble and grief.

6

Prisoners of the Third Reich

After a while we were taken back to Hamburg, at first briefly to the infamous police prison in the Huetten-strasse—a building that was later named for Helmuth Hueb-ener—then to Glasmoor, a kind of labor prison out in the bog country. There we were put to work cutting peat. We spaded the peat out in little loaf-shaped bricks and put it in the sun to dry so that it could be burned for fuel.

Duewer was put into the camp office, for our warden, *Oberregierungsrat* (senior government counsellor) Dr. Krueger, had told us from the first day we arrived there that he trusted us—he knew we were not criminals. The other men in the camp gave us a wide berth, however. They knew only that we'd been at the *Volksgerichtshof* and they called us *die Berliner,* the boys from Berlin. I think Dr. Krueger was secretly sympathetic toward us. He eventually got Rudi and me jobs in the tailor shop, and not long after that I became a kind of valet to the *Hauptwachtmeister,* the main guard in

The former Huetten prison in Hamburg. After the war it was renamed the
Helmuth Huebener Haus.

Karl-Heinz standing in a cell in the basement of the Huetten prison in 1984, forty-two years after he was incarcerated there.

The new Helmuth Huebener Haus in Hamburg, dedicated in 1984.

charge of the tailor shop. I cleaned his room and polished his
boots and made his bed. There was always a slice of bread on
his table for me when I'd finished.

After a while they gave me a job as a painter. I even had
my own little paint shop there, right outside the wall. Once
Dr. Krueger called me in and said, "Councilman So-and-so
wants his kitchen painted. Can we trust you to go there and
come back?" "Absolutely," I replied. He showed me the
way, and I walked for about an hour and a half through the
forest to get there. I painted the kitchen, and in the evening I
walked back. Running away was out of the question. I knew
they'd punish my family for it.

But life at Glasmoor was no picnic. We didn't get much
to eat, and we worked hard. And being in jail with hardened
criminal types was not much fun, either. We were the only
political prisoners there. For a while I had to share a cell with
a man who'd killed his own mother with an axe. He'd simply
chopped her head wide open. As a young boy who'd grown
up in a rather sheltered, religious home, I was horrified by
him. He always wanted to tell me about it.

"No, thanks," I'd say. "I don't want to hear it!"

"Why not?" he'd ask.

Some of the criminals there were murderers who'd run
away and joined the French Foreign Legion to escape prosecution. After the defeat of France, the Gestapo had asked the
Vichy government to send them all back. There were quite a
few of them at Glasmoor.

In August 1943 the Allies mounted terrible air raids
against Hamburg. The bombers attacked both day and night.
We could feel the earth tremble and could hear the distant
roar of the battle. During the first day we could see in the
distance over Hamburg what looked like great Christmas
trees covered with tinsel; this was the metal chaff that the
bombers dropped to confuse the anti-aircraft gunners on the

ground. At night the "Christmas trees" were replaced by lights and by the glow in the sky of the burning city. The next day the sun could not be seen, and it was almost totally blacked out for several more days. The ashes and the soot then began to settle out of the air, covering the ground all around us with a carpet of gray-black. Dr. Krueger had been in Hamburg, and he told us that our neighborhood of Hohenfelde had been completely leveled. I had no idea whether my family had somehow survived this holocaust— whether they had been evacuated or had hidden in our cellar or had been crushed or burned to death. Several more months were to pass before I heard that they were all safe. Only after the war did I learn that Helmuth's mother and both his grandparents had been killed in the raids. Hugo Huebener survived.

Parts of the prison camp at Glasmoor were cleared of inmates and turned over to refugees from Hamburg whose homes had been destroyed. Those of us who were "political prisoners" were entrusted with helping take food to them and arranging their living quarters.

We were at Glasmoor a little over a year, from August of 1942 until the end of 1943, just before Christmas. Then the three of us and some others with long sentences to serve were sent to Graudenz, a place on the Vistula River southeast of Danzig in present-day Poland, where they needed laborers. Dr. Krueger and his wife also happened to be transferred there at the same time. At Graudenz, the Air Force had constructed an underground aircraft factory where damaged ME 109 Messerschmitt fighter planes were dismantled and the good parts cleaned up and reassembled into new planes. The workers would take two or three wrecked planes and make one new one out of them.

As political prisoners we had to wear large yellow triangles painted on our backs and on our chests and on each leg of our trousers. These triangles were a bright, chrome yellow, visible a long way off.

We began by washing aircraft parts in powerful solvents which ate even the paint. Then I was given a job spray-painting the newly assembled planes. It was hard and dangerous work with all those chemicals, and we worked long days, usually at least twelve hours. Duewer, as usual, worked in the office there.

We lived above ground, just across the road from the factory in some old barracks surrounded by barbed wire and guarded by dogs. We had the usual bunks, two high. Our food was even worse than at Glasmoor. We had some cabbage and some soup, including one that Rudi and I particularly hated. We still ask each other, "Do you remember that soup that had sixty thousand eyes looking at you?" It was a fish soup full of little minnows, all still intact, uncleaned, and with their heads—and eyes—still in place. We got terrible stomachaches from that swill—but today we laugh about it.

I cannot say enough good about the Polish people with whom we worked there. They were really good to us, especially when they saw our yellow triangles, which told them that we were political prisoners and hence antifascists. One of them, Josef Ratzkowsky, I'll never forget. He worked on the planes with me, also spraying camouflage patterns on the barracks and roads in the area. He had bad teeth, most of the front ones being missing, and he looked like a real peasant. Josef was a fine man, who had contact with the Polish underground and offered to help me escape. "We have connections," he said. "We can let you disappear into congressional Poland" (which I took to be a code word for the underground). "We'll hide you, we'll keep you. You disappear. You are gone. We'll help you. Are you ready?" But I could never seriously consider escape. My parents had been in enough trouble already on my account. *Sippenhaft*, the arrest of one's relatives, was a principle well known and practiced in Nazi Germany.

But Josef gave me food and tobacco, for I had begun to smoke by this time, since it diminished the hunger pangs. And one time he said to me, "Tomorrow we have to go touch up a plane outside, where they hoist them up to synchronize the guns with the propeller. You come with me; we'll have a girl for you there. Her name is Maria. We'll leave you alone for twenty minutes and you have a little fun."

I blushed to the roots of my hair. "Sorry," I told him. "I don't do that. Not interested. It's very nice of you, but. . . ." I'd never had a girl or even really dated, and it never bothered me, then or later in Russia. However, when I returned to Hamburg in 1949 at the age of twenty-five, I realized how inexperienced I was with women. My social development had been arrested with me, and had no doubt even deteriorated since I had been sent to prison at the age of eighteen.

We were in Graudenz from December 1943 until January 1945, when the Russians broke through into East Prussia. When the word got out that the Russians were coming, panic spread among the German guards and the entire organization fell apart. Our factory was evacuated to the west, and we had to walk about two hundred miles, under guard, in January, in deep snow. Sometimes we heard a rumble behind us like distant thunder and we knew it was artillery. Every day the guards grew more friendly. Most of them could see that it was only a matter of time until *we'd* be guarding *them.*

Large groups of refugees joined us on the trek. Old women and children walked through the bitter cold and snow, carrying and pushing their belongings on small wagons or baby carriages. On the way we passed farms which had been abandoned by their owners. The cows, unmilked, stood bellowing in pain. I walked over to one of these abandoned farm buildings and took a horse, a harness, and a sleigh. We named the horse "Bel-ami" and put our belongings on the sleigh; our guards *Hauptwachtmeister* (master sergeant) Eggers, who also happened to be from Hamburg, and *Hauptwachtmeister* Jaeger, also put their things on. We began to form a kind of lifeboat friendship that was to save me a short time later.

The guards looked the other way while I went foraging for food for everyone in our group, and I managed to find quite a bit to eat on those farms. "Organizing," we called it. One late afternoon, I was out foraging when I heard a loud "Halt!" I turned around and there was a band of SS paratroopers. "Who are you? Your papers!"

"I don't have any papers."

"Put him up against this tree over here!" the lieutenant said. Just then Master-Sergeant Eggers came around the corner.

"Schnibbe," he said, "what are you doing here?"

"Do you know him?" the SS men asked.

"Yes. He belongs to me. Come with me, *schnell!*"

As soon as we were out of sight, Eggers turned the air blue with curses. *"Du dusseliger Hund! Was machst du da bloss fuer Geschichten!"* Another minute and I'd have been shot. It was a very close call. But we had to eat. The next day, out foraging again, I found half a pig someone had slaughtered and left unguarded for a moment. For our little group of about twenty-five people that pig was a very welcome treat.

Dr. Krueger and his wife were also among this group of several thousand refugees. They rode on a horse-drawn wagon loaded with their suitcases. By that time Dr. Krueger was not well and he couldn't walk, but since they were not walking, they suffered even more from the cold. No one was assigned to care for them, so I tried to locate them and take them something warm to eat and drink at the end of each day's march.

I was exhausted myself, usually, and sometimes I had to look all over the village for the Kruegers, but he had treated us like human beings at Glasmoor, and he had even saved our lives at Graudenz. When the Gestapo had requested that he send us to the concentration camp at Neuengamme, he had told them he needed our labor and could not spare us. He even showed us the Gestapo order. By helping them, I hoped to repay him for his kindness toward us. Later, after the war, I was subpoenaed to testify at his denazification hearing. When all the witnesses, including me, gave him a clean bill of health, he got back his high government job. He had managed to retain his character through the worst of times. He and his wife shook my hand after the hearing and we all had tears in our eyes.

On the trek there was a mother with two children. She put one child on the front of her bicycle and one on the back, and she pushed the bike along, since the snow was deep and the road congested. One evening we saw the mother, but not the children. "Where are the children?" we asked.

"Frozen. Dead," was her curt reply.

We often slept in school buildings. One night I went to sleep in a large auditorium filled with refugees, and there was a man next to me, rolled up tightly in his blanket. I spoke to him, but he didn't respond. *Boy, he's unsociable,* I thought. The next morning I spoke to him again, and then I touched him and saw that he'd been dead for days already.

Every so often a cry would run through the group: "Everybody off the road!" All the prisoners and refugees would roll their wagons and baby carriages and bikes off into the deeper snow and soon a small column of German tanks would roar through on their way east to try to stop the Russian advance. And then the refugees would struggle to get their things back up onto the road. Often they simply had to leave them there if they or the horses were too weak to get them out again.

One night, in an old schoolhouse, when Rudi and I were checking each other for frostbite, we couldn't find Gerhard.

"Where's Duewer?"

"I haven't seen him since this afternoon." We looked all around, and finally I started back the way we had come. I had to go almost six kilometers to find him. He was just sitting there in the snow. "I'll be right along," he said when he saw me. "I'm feeling fine. I just want to rest. I'm tired."

That was a very dangerous condition. I grabbed him and said, "You come with me right now."

He said, "Go ahead, I'll be right. . . ."

"No, no, no!" I helped him up and we both marched back to the school. The snow was so deep we had to waddle through it like geese.

Duewer froze his feet out there that night. From that point forward he had to ride on the sleigh. And later, when the recruiters combed through our camp inducting people into the army, they left him alone because of his feet and they took me.

We walked only about ten or twelve kilometers a day, for the roads were plugged with people. Eventually, however, near the end of March, after about three months on the road, we arrived just outside of Stettin, in Pomerania, East Germany. There were only a few guards left with us then, including Jaeger and Eggers. We were practically on our own. But we were still prisoners, and things got more organized again because we were near a large city. We were placed aboard a train, but before it could pull out, a bombing raid struck Stettin, and we had to wait several more days until the tracks were cleared.

Looking for food again, I stumbled into a camp of Russian POWs whose guards had deserted. They had stayed in place because it was the only safe thing to do. They gave me a milk can full of "soup," mostly hot water with a few vegetables floating in it. I got some help and we carried it back to the train. Little did I know that I would be in the Russians' situation within a few months, and that I would be living on such "soup" for four years!

The train moved away in the direction of Hamburg. I remember that it was a regular passenger train car, not a cattle car, because it had regular compartments with baggage nets overhead. We boosted poor Duewer up into the net so his feet would be out of the way and so that he could lie down. Our guard, who had found some liquor somewhere, was having a party with some women in the next car. He just locked us in and left us.

When we finally arrived in Hamburg, we were totally filthy and crawling with lice. After we went back to Glasmoor for delousing, we retrieved our old clothes—which German efficiency had kept there for us all this time!—and went to a camp called Hahnoefersand on an island out in the mouth of the Elbe River. It didn't need wire fences, since the nearest shore was four or five kilometers away, but it did have barracks like the other camps. We had only been there a short time when the recruiters came around. They wanted soldiers. We had fought against the *Reich* and been punished for it, but when they needed cannon fodder they were not too proud to take us. Rudi was not inducted because he had a longer sentence yet to serve, and Gerhard's feet were too bad. But I was available, and if I had said, "No, forget it," they'd have hanged me. So I went.

I was assigned to report to the Adolf Hitler Barracks in

Oldenburg. Since I now had civilian clothes again and my induction papers, I could go home on my way to the train station. My parents, who had been bombed out of their home in August of 1943, had moved into our garden house. Grandpa Luetkemueller had gone back to the relative safety of Luedelsen to stay with other relatives on the farm there. I hadn't seen them in almost three years; since I had left Graudenz they had not known where I was or even whether I was alive. (While I had been at Graudenz, Josef had smuggled letters out for me and mailed them to my parents.) But they had not been worried about me. "We didn't know where you were," Mom told me, "but somehow we knew you were safe."

Unfortunately, Dad was at work, but I had a wonderful, if very brief, reunion with Mom. "Don't you want to disappear into the rubble someplace here in Hamburg?" she said as I prepared to leave. "The war'll be over soon, and the town's full of deserters as it is."

If I'd known that the war was only going to last another four weeks, I think I'd have tried going underground somewhere. But having gone through what I had made me cautious. "I don't want to get knocked off by these guys at five minutes to twelve," I responded. "I'm going to play it safe." This decision meant that for me the war was to last another four years rather than four weeks.

So I took the next train to Oldenburg, though not before we sat out an air raid in Hamburg for several hours. We arrived late in Oldenburg, but then I just sat there in the barracks for two weeks. I was given no training, no uniform, no weapon. I just sat there.

7

The War
Ends

The Adolf Hitler Barracks were on a hill overlooking Oldenburg. One day there was a terrible air raid. We all watched from the air-raid trenches a few miles away as the four-engined B-17's dropped phosphorous and high explosives on Oldenburg. I have never seen anything like it in all my life. It seemed as though the whole sky was full of planes, looking like little silver fish. The pathfinder dropped a smoke flare and then a sound came like that of a huge organ with someone leaning on the keyboard. The air was full of the fury of war, and my spine tingled when I thought of Helmuth's predictions about the destruction of Germany. I was witnessing with my own eyes the death of a German city.

Evacuated from Oldenburg immediately after the raid, we were told to go to Tabor in Czechoslovakia to be attached to the *Armeegruppe Schoener*. But first we had to walk about forty kilometers to Bremen to find a railroad line that was still in operation. The forty kilometers would have been easy enough, but Allied fighter planes, *Jabos* [*Jagdbomber*] as we called them, were strafing all the streets, so we had to march along in two rows under the trees that lined the roads, where they couldn't see us as well. Every time we heard a plane we dived for cover. They'd strafe anything that moved, even livestock in the fields. And again I thought of Helmuth. Where was the mighty German Air Force now? The Allies had complete control of the air. Even though it was a deadly situation, I almost giggled, because I was struck by the irony of Hitler's prediction in 1933: "Give me ten years' time and you will not recognize Germany!" How true it was—though not in the way he had intended it.

As we walked along, we saw a large truck loaded with luggage and refugees. "Are you crazy?" we yelled out. "Where are you going?" They had a man sitting on each fender and one on the back, and when one of these lookouts saw a plane the truck stopped and everyone scattered into the woods. But as they drove past us and went out of sight around a corner, we heard a fighter plane peel off and dive at them with its engine howling. Then we heard its guns firing. When we got around the corner, we could not believe the mess we saw. Corpses littered the road and the truck was all shot to bits. It was awful.

In Bremen, right near the station, we were caught in another air raid. It was unsafe to walk in Germany day or night, city or country. Finally our train left for Tabor, and we actually made it to Czechoslovakia. I now wish we had been more delayed by the air raids. By then it was around the twentieth or twenty-fifth of April, only two weeks before the capitulation. I sat around in the barracks for a while longer, still with no weapon, though I had been given a uniform by now, and we listened to pep talks by the unit's propaganda officer and played soccer with the little Czech kids from the neighborhood. Those who had received uniforms traded their civilian clothes to a local grocer for tobacco or food. He knew that in a few weeks he could sell them for just about any price to someone who wanted badly to get out of a German uniform.

One morning we were ordered to march west. We hadn't gone far when we came to a bridge guarded by four Russian tanks. While we had been playing soccer in Tabor, the Russians had encircled us! Our officers put their heads together. Should we attack, or should we surrender? We surrendered. The Germans who had rifles just smashed them to bits against concrete house corners or on the pavement and threw them away.

The Russians herded us into a big meadow, put guards around us, and told us to lie down for the night. Every few minutes one of them would fire a burst of tracer bullets, angry little glowworms, over us, about four feet off the ground, to keep us from raising our heads or walking away. The next day we were marched back east—back into Czechoslovakia.

May of 1945 was an unusually hot, dry month. The Czechs stood in front of their wells to keep the Germans from getting water. They had gathered up some German rifles and pistols, and they were very abusive. I understood why they were angry; I had heard about the village of Lidice, which had been annihilated by the Germans, and I knew that many Czechs had suffered in the camps. At first the Russians and the Czechs seemed to celebrate the victory together, but after a few days the Russians seemed to be taking what they wanted—women, livestock, and food— and the mood changed.

On the third day of our trek several Germans got sunstroke, and we put them under a tree in the shade. We asked a Czechoslovakian farmer for some water, but he chased us away and set his big dog on us. Three of us decided to stay with the sick men and help them if we could. Then two Russian soldiers appeared, and we told them our story.

To our surprise, one of them spoke excellent German. "Follow me," he said, when he'd heard enough. We went back to the farmer, who immediately started cursing the Russians, too, for "not letting the damn Germans croak." They asked him for water, and he refused again. Finally, the Russians lost their patience with him. One of them hit him two or three times in the face with his fist; meanwhile, the other Russian shot the dog with his machine gun and then pointed the gun at the farmer and his family. His comrade took us into the barn and got a horse, a harness, and a wagon, and told us to hitch up. All of the sick soldiers were loaded up, and away we went for Tabor. There are good and bad in every country; this time the Russians were the good guys. Those two soldiers saved quite a few German lives that day.

Every so often a Russian tank column came zooming along at full speed, heading for Prague. Sometimes they'd screech to a halt and yell down at us, *"Hitler kaputt!"* Then they'd throw down cigarettes or a bottle of wine and tear away again in a cloud of smoke. They were usually about half drunk, and totally euphoric about the victory.

Once an SS column came down the road at top speed in their vehicles, trying to break through the Russian lines. They were justifiably afraid the Russians and the Czechs would kill them if they were captured, so they were roaring along, firing their guns in all directions. We heard them coming and dived for cover in the ditch beside the road. A gunfight ensued which lasted only a few minutes. When it was over, the area was littered with the corpses of SS men.

The Czechs were already taking items off their bodies. I was horrified. Would this nightmare ever end?

Along the route back to Tabor, we arrived at the site of a large German motor pool. There were hundreds of German trucks of all descriptions there—Horchs, Buessings, and Mercedes—covered with tarpaulins. Just as we arrived, another tank column rolled up. A Russian officer jumped down from his tank, grabbed one of the men in our group, and began to kick him. Not knowing what was happening, we retreated a few steps. Then the Russian took his machine gun and fired several vertical bursts into the man's body. The man fell dead right before our eyes, about eight or ten feet from me. He turned out to be a Russian who had fought under General Vlasov on the German side. How they knew him I haven't the slightest idea, unless it was from the markings on his uniform.

No sooner had this horrible thing happened than a Russian soldier came up to me, poked me with the butt of his gun, and motioned for me to follow him. *"Idi siuda!"* I played dumb, but he pulled me over into a line of trucks. He marched along behind me with his gun while I thought, *Oh, my gosh, now it's my turn!* He steered me this way and that —then he stopped me at one particular truck. *"Stoi!"* He motioned for me to pull back the tarp and climb in. When I looked inside the truck, I saw that it was full of hard German salami, big white beauties, as big as a man's arm. I loaded as many as I could carry and marched back to my comrades. My Russian was laughing and having a really good time helping us to find food. And I thought he had wanted to kill me!

There was, in fact, a problem with food in Tabor. The Czech bakers refused to bake bread for the hated Germans. One morning the Russians arrested all the bakers in town;

then the whole population was without. After that they baked for everyone.

The Russians divided us up into commandos—work details—and we had to clear up ammunition. The Germans had left live ammo—88- and 105-millimeter shells—lying everywhere; it was a serious danger to the populace. So we worked carrying rounds to a large pit, where they were detonated. One detail I worked on was in charge of stealing sewing machines. Our Russian loved sewing machines, especially the German ones. He took us from house to house, and when we found a good machine, we "liberated" it and carried it out to his truck. Inferior ones he made us throw out of the window onto the pavement.

Another Russian liked discipline: he made his commandos march and sing German army songs. The Czechs hated it, but he kept them quiet with his gun while we marched and sang. He laughed.

Then one Russian ordered the Germans to beat up some Czech teenagers who were hanging around and who had thrown some rocks at us. The Germans caught them and beat them up while the Russians held their guns on them. The war was over, and their euphoria made them do strange things!

The Czechs were beginning to see that they might have driven out the devil with Beelzebub. They began to tell us how they disliked the Russians. One of our Czech guards came on duty one day with a long face. Four or five Russians had raped his wife. "I help them guard you and they rape my wife," he fumed. "As far as I'm concerned, you can all go home right now!"

And, of course, every day the Russians said, *"Skoro domoi"* ("Tomorrow you go home"). We believed them. The war was over. What point was there in keeping prisoners? Then one day it seemed to be coming true; we were called up, our heads were shaved, we were deloused, and our clothes were placed in big, hot delousing ovens. I was a bit suspicious, though. *Why delouse us just to turn us loose?* I wondered. We sat there in the camp for one more day, and then they loaded us onto a cattle train and it pulled out. *Hurrah,* we thought. *We're going home!*

8

Out of the Frying Pan . . .

It was in June of 1945 when we were deloused, shaved, and placed in boxcars in Tabor, Czechoslovakia. There were from six thousand to eight thousand German POWs there, and the ground water was becoming contaminated from all the latrines. The Czechs wanted us moved, and the Russians finally obliged.

We were completely disoriented in the boxcars. We couldn't tell whether we were going north toward Germany or not. Then all of a sudden someone spotted a sign reading *"Wien."* "Vienna! We are not going home. That's the other way!" Beyond Vienna we entered Hungary. We were on our way to the Soviet Union.

Every two days or so the train stopped and the guards threw some bread in to us—very little per man—and some salted fish. We had very little water. The cars were crowded but we could lie down, though there was no straw. The doors on one side were blocked open slightly, and two boards had been nailed together in a V-shaped trough which ran outside at an incline. This was our urinal. To defecate, we had to wait for the next rest stop.

Many of the men began to complain of the treatment, but I had heard of Germans transporting Russian prisoners in midwinter on open cars, so I was less concerned. And though I was a prisoner again, the last thing in the world I wanted to be, at least I was not being punched and kicked by the SS and the Gestapo. Then, too, my Nazi imprisonment had made me more able than most to endure difficult conditions with little food. So I kept quiet and let the others complain. Some of them were still quite pro-Hitler, as well, so I didn't dare say anything about my antifascist past, either. "Oh, you're one of those who stabbed us in the back, huh?" they would have said. "You guys made us lose the war!"

We travelled for what seemed an eternity, stopping very often on sidings while troop transports rolled by. The journey must have actually lasted for about three or four weeks, however, with stops for two days in Romania where we waited for another train (my overriding impression there was olfactory, of the omnipresent garlic) and in Brest-Litovsk, where we changed to the wider-gauge railroad of the Soviet Union.

One day the train stopped near an enormously wide river, and two men from each car were ordered out to go for water. Since I was sitting near the door, I fell right out and ran down to the river. I was so thirsty and dirty and tired that I just plunged in and began to drink. The water was filthy, but I didn't care. I just brushed back the surface scum and drank and drank. Later I learned that this was the Volga. We had reached our destination. When we had finished drinking, we carried water to the train. Soon we all had diarrhea from the dirty water.

Not far from this place on the river, the train stopped

again, right in the middle of nowhere, out in the steppes, and we got out. The train puffed away, and we were left alone there in the hot wind.

We began to march. When we had gone a mile or two, we saw four watchtowers with barbed wire strung between them. There was nothing else there but weeds, three or four feet high, and a pile of building materials; prefabricated German barracks that had apparently been shipped to that place just before we arrived. We were told to get to work assembling the barracks if we wanted to be warm and dry. We rolled up our sleeves and set to work.

Suddenly some civilians appeared, around forty or fifty of them, mostly women, who all spoke German—that is to say, a Swabian dialect of German. We were completely perplexed about where they'd come from until we learned that these were the Volga Germans, descendents of people who'd emigrated to Russia from near Stuttgart more than a century before, when Catherine the Great had given them homesteads there. They all lived in the next hamlet, Bokhvisnevo. They had dugout houses covered with earth and with one exposed wall, containing a window and a door, facing south. A stovepipe stuck up out of the mound of earth. Today we would say they lived in very effective passive solar, earth-insulated homes! A few steps led down into a panelled corridor and then into their very clean, very cozy rooms.

Most of the men were gone, conscripted into the Red Army and killed or missing in action. I began to understand why we had been brought to Russia: our labor was to replace that of the men who'd been killed. We who had destroyed Russia were to help rebuild her.

Our camp commandant told us that we'd get three days off if we'd build the camp in two weeks. We built furiously, but we didn't get any time off. We dug deep footings and mixed concrete and poured foundations. We made a kind of concrete block and built walls out of those. We had a lot of tradesmen in our group of about three thousand—carpenters, masons, plumbers—and they got things done right. We built barracks for sleeping, and one for a kitchen, and one for a bakery, and one for a pantry or storehouse, and one for an infirmary, and one for the German officers, and one outside the wire for the camp commandant, and another for the Russian officers. We constructed little picnic tables in front of each barrack to eat on in the summer months. There were latrines, each with a long piece of wood to sit on, and there was a tap outside each barrack with water running out of it all the time.

The barbed-wire enclosure was about twelve feet high, but it was not electrified. There was a shorter wire fence just inside the big fence; between them was the no-man's-land. Over the main gate was one light bulb which burned day and night. There was also a loudspeaker that aroused us for roll call. In short, it was a typical labor camp. All the other camps looked very much the same.

If *"skoro domoi"* ("you're going home soon") was the first Russian expression we learned, *"rabotai"* ("work!") was the second, and *"davai"* ("hurry up!") was the third. We were there as laborers, and labor we did. Since Bokhvisnevo was in a gas- and oil-producing region, we dug trenches for pipelines and built pumping stations. There was so much petroleum in the ground there that the whole area smelled bad, like rotten eggs, the water tasted oily until we got used to it, and gas and oil actually bubbled out of the ground. We pushed an old piece of drilling pipe down into one of these gas vents and rigged a burner in our barracks out of a larger piece of pipe which was attached to a chimney. Our makeshift heater roared and turned red-hot and kept us warm at night all through the long Russian winter. Some of the crude oil in that place was so fine that they burned it directly in diesel trucks without refining it in any way.

We arrived at Bokhvisnevo in early August of 1945. At the end of September, it began to snow. I've never seen so much snow in my life. It was four or five feet deep on the level, with drifts ten to twelve feet deep everywhere. It was also bitter cold. Trees would freeze solid and split right down the middle. Temperatures of forty-five degrees below zero were not uncommon. Often we'd be rousted out on a snowy morning and marched back up to the train line to shovel snow off the tracks. We cleared one section of track, and POWs from one of the many other camps in the area cleared the next. This was, as I learned, the line into Kuyby-shev and on into the Ural Mountains and then to Siberia.

When the tracks were cleared, we returned to our trenches. Though the ground was frozen, we still had to peck away at it every day. Some days we only dug out a few handfuls of frozen dirt all day. The trenches had to be very deep, about eight feet, apparently so that the pipe would be below the frostline. In the summer, when the ground was not frozen, we had to taper each side so that it wouldn't cave in on us. In the winter we tried to get down as deep as pos-sible in the trench, out of the fierce east winds, and we sort of tunnelled along the bottom. We had large sledgehammers and chisels for chipping away at the frozen ground; one man held the chisel, and another hit it with the hammer. We be-came quite skilled at hitting it just right so that a crack de-veloped, releasing a chunk of frozen dirt that we could throw out of the trench in one piece.

Until 1946, when I got warmer clothes—the padded jacket, fur cap, and warm felt boots called *valenkis* which never got wet because it never thawed all winter—all I had was the uniform I'd had on when I was captured. There were days when we just hopped up and down all day in the trench trying to keep warm and watched out for frostbite on each other's ears and noses. Each winter some of our people lost fingers and toes to frostbite. Often the Russians punished them when that happened, because they suspected it was intentional mutilation to get out of working.

There were other camps in the area containing *zakliuch-ionnyes*, Russian civilians who'd been sentenced to a labor camp for some infraction. This was part of the infamous *Gulag* system. There were also, strangely enough, camps of former Russian soldiers who had been POWs in Germany. They were being "re-educated," we were told, after having seen the West and having been exposed to western propaganda. Sometimes we worked next to each other on adjoining sections of trench.

Our diet consisted of 500 grams—about one pound—of bread for the day, which we got in the morning. It was black bread, so slimy and gooey that we used to say you could throw it on the wall and it would stick, although no one ever wasted any actually trying. At noon and again in the evening we got the same kind of cabbage soup, *kapusta*. We called it *Rundfunksuppe* (radio soup,) because of the slogan *"Wir melden uns gleich wieder"* ("we'll be right back.") Not only did the hunger come right back; this *kapusta* itself was like water, and it went right through. Sometimes there was fish in it, and sometimes it contained a few potatoes. It was never clean; there was always a sandy, gritty residue at the bottom. The Russians stored the potatoes outside in the winter, frozen as solid as rocks. *"Nichevo,"* they'd say. "It doesn't matter." Then they defrosted the potatoes and dumped the slimy, black things into the soup. We also got a kind of malt coffee to drink, to which we applied various crude and unappetizing euphemisms.

We were always so hungry, however, that we didn't care how bad the food tasted or what unappetizing names we had for it. And we knew that the Russians didn't really eat much better than we did. They were trying to rebuild their economy and had to tighten their belts as well. We did have one good dish, *kasha,* a gruel made with millet. We got one scoop of that in the evening, and it was quite a treat.

But it was never enough. We were all really slowly starving to death. When I was released I weighed 49 kilos — about 104 pounds — on a 6-foot-2-inch frame. There were many, many deaths in the camps from malnutrition and related diseases like *dystrophica,* a kind of edema or accumulation of water in the tissues due to starvation. Every two months or so we all had to strip and parade naked in front of a Russian medical commission, almost always comprised of women doctors. They looked at one thing: our buttocks. If these were at all round, if there was still any fat there, we were okay. Anyone whose buttocks were too thin was not fit to work and might be sent home.

I became well acquainted with one of these Russian doctors, as well as with a German doctor who came to our camp. One night I was told to go with a guard and another prisoner to Bokhvisnevo and pick up a German *vrach,* a doctor. We walked the three miles or so and picked him up at about eleven. I'll never forget how cold it was. The air was so clear that the stars looked as though we could reach up and touch them. Trees were freezing and exploding, and there were wolves howling in the countryside around us.

9

Russia
and Russians

The German doctor's name was Georg Wille; since he was from Schleswig-Holstein, we had the same low-German dialect in common and hit it off immediately. He was an *Oberstabsarzt*, a high-ranking medical officer who'd been with the German army in Russia and had been captured. Since our camp needed a German doctor to assist the Russian doctor, he'd been sent there from an officers' camp. He did all the minor work, such as lancing carbuncles. We had an epidemic of carbuncles—from our filthy diet, no doubt, and also perhaps from the lice and the bedbugs. We also had typhoid with cholera-type diarrhea.

Our Russian doctor was named Tanya. She was very young, perhaps twenty-four or twenty-five, but she was a doctor of medicine with the rank of lieutenant. She was assigned to our camp to work with Dr. Wille. All the medical supplies for our camp were in a government warehouse out past Kuybyshev, the nearest large town. Tanya

had to go there every three or four months to pick up supplies; on several occasions she happened to choose me to go
with her and help her load them onto the truck. I didn't
know what had drawn her attention to me; I just remember
her stopping me in the camp and telling me to pack my
things because we were going on a trip. We had a truck and
a driver and two big barrels of fuel in the truck to enable us
to reach Kuybyshev, about four hundred miles away.

We drove cross-country through the steppes, travelling
mostly along a little dirt trail where two tire tracks were
visible in the grass. I rode in the back, and Tanya and the
driver were in the cab. When we got out of sight of the
camp, however, the truck stopped and she climbed into the
back with me. She wanted to practice her German, which
she had learned in occupied Germany. We agreed to speak
German for an hour and then Russian for an hour.

When we started to converse she asked me to tell her
about myself—where I was from, what I did at home, who
my parents were, and what my father did. But before I could
reply, she suddenly blurted out, "Are you a Nazi?" I denied
it with a clear conscience. But she was not very impressed,
since she'd doubtless heard that from every German POW.

Then she asked me if I believed in God. And I said,
"Yes, I do." Then she said, "So do I." I almost fell off the
truck. I said, "I don't believe you."

She replied, "Why not?"

"You are a Russian officer. Russian officers don't believe
in God. Religion is the opiate of the people isn't it?"

But she insisted that she believed in God and said, "Tell
me about your God." I tried, in a very clumsy way, to tell
her about my faith. I now wish I had been more knowledge-
able and informed about the gospel.

After she had listened to my explanations, I asked her,
"Now, why did you choose me? You have medics who help

you. Why didn't you take one of them? Or why not just use your driver to help you?" She said, "I saw you and you seemed different."

She was a pretty girl, tall, with blond hair and blue eyes. She was from Siberia, but she had lost contact with her family during the war. She was sure that her father and brother had been killed in action. Our friendship began to grow, but it remained platonic. I was very emaciated and sick and had no interest at all in any kind of physical love. I was a Mormon boy who had never touched or even kissed a girl! Tanya also seemed to be more interested in a spiritual rather than a physical relationship.

Much later we began to have entertainments at the camp, a variety show or a concert, every two weeks or so. Among those thousands of people, there were many talented, professional entertainers, such as Kurt Engels, a tenor from the Dresden opera. The prisoners worked thousands of extra hours to buy the instruments for our orchestra. When I went to one of these concerts, there sat Tanya, in one of the first four rows which were reserved for Russian officers. She was wearing a beautiful wine-red dress; when she got up and moved back to sit next to me, the other POWs whistled and stomped their feet. I was very shy and very inexperienced with women, so naturally I blushed until my face matched her dress. I was terribly embarrassed and befuddled, but she was greatly amused. *"Nichevo,"* she said, "it doesn't matter."

On one of our trips for medical supplies she suddenly got up, banged on the cab of the truck, and told the driver to stop. *"Stoi!"* We came to a halt right by a beautiful little river at the edge of a big, deep forest that the Russians call the *taiga*.

"Let's take a break here," Tanya said to the driver.

"Okay." The driver lay down on the seat, hung his legs out of the window, and took a nap.

"Let's swim," she said to me.

I replied, "I don't have any swimming trunks."

"So what?" she asked. The Russians are very open, I found. So we stripped down to our underwear and plunged into the river.

After we'd swum for a while I had to relieve myself, so I swam across the river and walked twelve or fifteen feet into the *taiga*. That was a big mistake. I was immediately attacked by mosquitoes. It was unbelievable. I have never seen so many mosquitoes, or such big ones! After that trip I got sick with *volinien* fever, which I must have caught from those mosquitoes. It's a lot like malaria, which I was to catch later on. Tanya took care of me, coming to the infirmary every day and sitting with me until I had recovered some. Then she arranged for me to be sent for a few days to a collective farm, a *kolkhoz*, for recuperation.

Every morning a farmer picked me up on his way to the *kolkhoz* with his scruffy little horse wagon. We travelled about an hour. Then I just sat in the sun and ate *kasha* and drank sour milk. Tanya occasionally came out during the day to check on me. Once she brought some tackle with her, and we went fishing. She was a very enterprising woman. We didn't catch anything, but we had fun.

We sometimes received German newspapers in the camp, though they were almost a year old. One day we got one from Berlin that had an article about the German resistance movement. Our group was mentioned. I took the paper to Tanya and proudly showed her the photograph of Helmuth, Rudi, and me; our names were also mentioned in the article. Then she believed what I'd told her about my not being a Nazi.

Later on, for the last two years or so, we had our Sundays free. Then the POWs just sat around the camp and took naps or went to the antifascist indoctrination lectures. I never volunteered, because whenever I told a Russian that I

was an antifascist—even after I showed them the article—
they often replied, "Well, then, why are you still alive? Why
didn't you blow Hitler up or at least throw yourself in front
of his train?" Those POWs who were Marxist-Leninist from
before, or who were converted to it by these lectures were
sent to other indoctrination camps and then on to Moscow,
where they received further schooling and joined the "Com-
mittee for a Free Germany" before being sent home to the
German Democratic Republic to help further the cause.

After about two years, in the summer of 1947, I was
moved near Yablonka to a larger camp of about five or six
thousand, right near the Volga. Luckily for me, both our
camp doctors, Tanya and Georg Wille, were also transferred
with our group. Enormous floats or rafts of logs from the
forests in the north had arrived at Yablonka, and we were
needed to fish them out of the river. These floats were sometimes a mile and a half long and half a mile wide, with the
logs all chained together around the edges. The Volga boat-
men—and they do sing their famous songs, I discovered—
who floated the logs downstream had built little houses on
them, with stoves and everything. They even brought their
families. They steered these rafts with big rudders at the
back.

When the rafts were tied fast, we began pulling the logs
out to be taken to a sawmill. We made huge mountains of
logs. We had some German Maybach half-tracks with
winches in front which we parked along the shore, facing the
river. Then we constructed a skidway out of two parallel
lines of logs running from the river up onto the shore. We
spooled out the cable down to the shore, tied twenty or so
logs together, and pulled this bundle up crosswise to the
skid rails.

Once, when I was standing there watching a load of
logs slide by, the cable suddenly snapped. The broken end
lashed out and hit a man standing very near to me. He was

literally cut in halves where he stood. As he died he looked amazed, as if he could not understand what had hit him.

The worst accidents, of course, were in those camps in the *taiga* where the logs were cut. We heard hair-raising stories of people being crushed by trees and made deathly ill by mosquitoes.

After the logs were all hauled up, we were put to work building a town for oil workers. Since we built a brick school and some brick houses, I was a hod carrier. Later, when I saw the film of Solzhenitsyn's "One Day In The Life Of Ivan Denisovich," I was immediately transported back to my hod-carrying days in Yablonka, the oil town.

In the wintertime we had to build a fire under the sand we used to make mortar. The mason would put this steaming hot mortar on the brick and plop it into place. It had to be exactly in the right position, for it froze down immediately. There was no moving it after that.

We hod carriers had a device for transporting mortar that looked like a stretcher or a sedan chair. It had two handles in front and two behind. I was working with a young music student and I was on the back. I had just stumbled over a brick or something when I got a strong desire to change places with him.

"I can't see where I'm stepping here on the back," I said. "Why don't you trade with me for a while?"

"Okay," he replied. We exchanged ends and started out. We hadn't gotten ten feet when he fell down. I thought he'd stumbled; I turned around to say, "See, it's not so easy there, is it?" Then I saw blood gushing out of his neck. A Mongolian guard, for some reason, had decided to use him for target practice. We had not heard the shot. Someone called for the doctor, but the music student was dead. The Mongolian just stood by, grinning, and said, *"Kamerad kaputt!"*

The other guards may have feared a riot, because they grabbed him, took away his gun, and hustled him off. He was never seen in our camp again. No one knew if he'd been court-martialled or merely transferred.

After this incident, I began to feel as though someone was watching over me. I felt regret that the music student had been killed, but I realized that it could just as easily have been me. I began to be more religious, praying openly when I had a chance and to myself when there were others around. I thanked the Lord for every day that I was allowed to live. I thanked him for sending Tanya and Dr. Wille to me. They saved my life several times—but one particularly dramatic example stands out in my mind.

I was very sick with an attack of malaria which I had picked up along the Volga. It was not the tropical variety, apparently, but the kind we called *"tezerna."* I became very tired and I finally just couldn't move anymore. "You'd better rest," Dr. Wille said. "I'm putting you in the infirmary." Then, after a day or two, he stopped by my cot. "What do you want?" he asked.

"What do you mean, what do you want?" I replied.

"You called my name as I walked by," he told me.

"No, I didn't."

"Oh, come on," he insisted. "I heard my name! You called me." Looking at me more closely, he felt my pulse; then he rushed out, returning immediately with a syringe full of camphor, with which he injected me.

Later, when this crisis had passed, he said, "You know, my friend, your heart was very, very faint, very weak. We almost lost you there." He had been caring for several hundred patients that day. I cannot believe that he'd have had time to check on me if he had not thought he'd heard me calling out his name as he went by.

It took me a long time to recuperate from the malaria. In fact, I never did completely recover until later, after I'd been released. I'd lie in bed for three days with chills and then a fever. Later I'd feel better for about four weeks, and then I'd get the chills and the shakes again. I could tell when an attack was coming on, because I felt just as one does when one gets up in the morning and has to stretch. Then the next day, just like clockwork, I'd be sick again for about three days. Even with five blankets I couldn't keep warm.

While I was recuperating I had to help with the burial detail. There were many deaths there—1,110,000 in all the camps, to be exact—some of them caused by prisoners eating large quantities of salt so that they could get sick enough to be sent home. The salt made them retain water, their legs swelled up, and soon many of them died of congestive heart failure. Dr. Wille, who performed the autopsies, told me what had happened. Three of us and a driver would drive a load of corpses out into the steppes, dig a mass grave, and place the bodies in it, all naked, with no coffins. We were a bit sentimental, so we always tried to bury them facing west, facing home. And we made little crosses of sticks and placed a few wild flowers on the graves if we could find some.

In the fall we all had to go out into the countryside and help with the harvest, particularly potatoes, on the collective farms. There was a very short growing season there and the winter always came very early, so there was very little time after the potatoes ripened and before the ground froze. We had to work like mad for a week or two. But the soil there was beautiful, and the crops were good. The Russians often neglected to dig out all the potatoes in each hill—they merely wanted to fill their quota—so we POWs got permission to glean out the rest of the potatoes. When the Russians saw the small mountain we accumulated, they came and hauled them away.

One time we travelled about six hours by truck out to a collective farm. We had, as usual, a barrel of gasoline on the back of the truck. It somehow sprang a tiny leak, which saturated the rough boards on which one of our buddies sat. He didn't notice it, and when we arrived, the skin on his buttocks was completely raw. There were blisters as big as eggs. It had already begun to smell bad and to exude pus. Nothing we did seemed to offer him any relief. He just lay there on his belly in agony.

We asked the Russians for help. Soon an old grandma, a *babushka*, came over. She must have been a hundred years old. She found an old rotten fence post, scraped out some of the rotten wood, took it home, dried it over her stove, rubbed it into a powder, and wanted to sprinkle it on our friend's bottom.

"Bah; that's baloney," he said.

"Well, it can't hurt," we told him. So she went ahead and sprinkled it on the wound. I don't know whether there was some natural antibiotic in the wood mold or what, but the next day the wound had scabbed over, and it quickly healed thereafter.

While we were there, I got another attack of diarrhea. I was in pain with cramps and a stomachache. This same old woman took me into her house, where there was a big stove that people actually slept on and chickens and pigs running around underfoot, and then she climbed up a ladder into a loft, descending with some little paprika peppers. She went to the stove, where she had a pot of pumpkin soup bubbling. She consulted a big old book written in Tartar or something —I know this sounds like a fairy tale—and then she put the peppers into the soup, waving them back and forth through it, all the while bending up and down in a rhythmical way and chanting. She put some of this soup in a bowl and told me to eat it. It was very hot, but she made me eat it all. The next day my diarrhea was gone, my cramps were gone; I felt good again. I have never since scoffed at folk cures.

Every Russian I met there had healthy teeth, strong and white. Perhaps their water had fluoride in it, or perhaps it was the lack of sugar in their diet; I don't know. I'm certain that it was not from brushing their teeth, because when we first arrived in Russia and still had toothbrushes, the Russians and the Volga Germans would come to the camp fence every morning to watch in amazement as we brushed our teeth at the tap outside our barracks. They'd never seen anything quite like that.

As I've said, the Russians certainly didn't have too much to eat. The German invasion and the war had so ruined their economy that they really didn't have much more than we did, especially in 1945 and 1946. They were not allowed to keep cows and chickens, or, if they were, the state took most of the milk, butter, and eggs. They did have little garden plots behind their houses, however, and they grew vegetables there and a native tobacco called *makhorka*. Every spring the Russians gathered the wild onions which grew in abundance in the area, and berries and other edible things of the steppes and forests. There is nothing more beautiful, incidentally, than the steppes in springtime. Overnight they turn into a purple carpet, stretching for miles in every direction. The wild flowers only last a few days, of course, and then the onions take over. Everywhere you go you can smell them.

These Russians were good-hearted people. Often an old woman would cry when she saw us. "Why are you crying, *Matka?*" someone would ask. "Well, I have to think of your mother and how much she misses you." They were never cruel to us; they never taunted us or threw rocks. Of course, most of them had never seen the fighting; they were too far to the east. They thought all Germans had horns, and when they saw us we looked just like their sons.

There were very few men left, but the women were amazingly strong and hardworking. They worked on roads and in the fields, wearing their shoes of woven tree bark and with rags wrapped around their legs. Their heads were always covered with scarves, and they wore the same quilted clothing winter and summer.

From Yablonka we went temporarily to Ufa and Saratov, as our labor was needed there. In Saratov, a place about seven hundred kilometers southeast of Moscow, there were trains of hopper cars loaded with coal that needed unloading. We pulled the handles on the cars and the coal spilled out the bottom. We shovelled it onto the same kind of two-man stretchers we had used to transport mortar in Yablonka and dumped it onto a big pile near the tracks. We worked around the clock there; I had the night shift. Even though we were doing it by hand and we were all very weak, several thousand men working around the clock can unload a lot of coal.

Next we unloaded flour, and then heavy machinery from Germany. The Russians were dismantling factories in East Germany as reparation payments and shipping the machines to the Soviet Union. We unloaded boxcars full of precision tools, lathes, generators, engines, and machines of all kinds, and just piled them on the ground, since there was no place to store them. In a few months they had been ruined by the rain and snow.

The POWs were, by and large, very cooperative and very helpful to each other; we were all weak and trying to survive, and there existed a kind of lifeboat camaraderie. But once or twice we had a real mean type in the camp. One was our German camp commander. His name was, appropriately enough, Adolf. He was from a German-speaking province on the Russian border, Latvia or Lithuania or someplace, who spoke fluent Russian. He organized a kind of protection racket, shaking down the prisoners for any valuables they might have managed to hang onto. These he traded to the Russians for vodka. One of his jobs in the camp was to organize baths at the public sauna down at the village where we bathed once a month or so. While he was there he got a Russian girl pregnant, so they simply kept him there and made him marry the girl. It was a machine-gun wedding, so to speak. He never was allowed to go home.

Another POW was a loudmouth who was always screaming and yelling at people. We called him *nachalnik,* "administrator," because he was so pushy, always throwing his weight around and giving orders. He spoke fluent Russian, too. Then one day he was gone. No one knew where he was; nobody said anything. Two days later the whole camp was assembled outside for roll call. The camp commander came and read a statement to the effect that this man was a Russian who had been taken prisoner by the Germans right at the beginning of the war and had collaborated with them and had even been in charge of a camp of Russian POWs! He had been executed at five o'clock that morning, the commander said. We all thought the man had been pretty stupid to call attention to himself by being such a loudmouth.

Meanwhile, I was getting so weak that Dr. Wille arranged to have me assigned to the bakery, a great place to work because I could eat as much as I wanted. When I arrived there these relatively healthy, strong bakers made me scrub my hands, and then they told me to knead the dough. There was a large trough there, about twenty feet long, full of flour and water and leavening. I put my arms into the dough and got them immediately stuck. I was simply too weak to pull them out. The bakers were very amused. "Come on," they said as they pulled me out, "eat something first."

I worked there about a month, but then I made a mistake and I got myself driven out of this paradise. I'd met a young man whose last name I've now forgotten, but whose first name, Helmuth, for obvious reasons I remember well. While I was at the bakery, the Russians discovered that he'd been a member of the *Leibstandarde Adolf Hitler*, the body-guards of Adolf Hitler, an elite SS unit. Actually, only a few of these *LAH* men were Hitler's guards; the rest were simply soldiers and their unit designation a supposedly honorary one. But the Russians didn't like the SS at all, and they'd peri-odically throw Helmuth into the stockade for questioning.

This barrack had a high, open window, so when I walked by on my way to my barrack from the night shift, I could ask Helmuth how he was doing. When I heard he was not being fed very much, I began taking half a loaf of bread with me and tossing it through that window every morning. One morning the Russian political officer was in there with Helmuth and the bread practically landed in his lap! My days as a baker were over. It was back to the Volga, pulling out logs. Within a few weeks I lost all the weight I had gained in the bakery.

But Tanya had a girl friend there, Tamara, the camp *perevodchik*, the interpreter. Tanya told Tamara that I was trustworthy, so Tamara took me with her on the train to Kuybyshev, where she had to pick up some paper forms and other office supplies from a government printing office. In Russia everything had to be officially filled out in triplicate, so we went through a lot of paper. Tamara happened to be from Kuybyshev, so she took me to meet her parents. They were very nice people, and Tamara was a very nice girl. She den 12. 12. 48.

Meine lieben Eltern und Geschwister!
Wie oft werde ich Euch noch schreiben? Ich hätte nie
geglaubt jetzt noch hier sein zu müssen, aber immer
wieder habe ich mich geirrt. Nun hoffe ich wieder,
dass es das letzte mal sein wird, wo ich an Euch
schreibe. Weihnachten steht wieder vor der Tür. Wie gerne
wäre ich im Kreise meiner Lieben, die ich schon so
lange entbehrt und vermisst habe, aber das Schicksal
ist grausam hart, es fragt nicht nach den Wünschen
und Nöten der Menschen. Es muss wohl so sein, denn
sonst wäre es nicht so. Aber ich will nicht versagen, sondern
weiter ausharren, denn einmal wird es doch Frühling
werden und dann gibt es ein Glücklich sein ohne Ende.
Wie geht es Euch sonst? Hoffentlich immer noch gut. Von
mir das Gleiche. Nun seid alle recht herzlichst gegrüßt
Euer immer an Euch denkender Sohn und Bruder Karl-Hein...

СОЮЗ ОБЩЕСТВ КРАСНОГО КРЕСТА и КРАСНОГО ПОЛУМЕСЯЦА
СССР

Почтовая карточка военнопленного
Carte postale du prisonnier de guerre

Бесплатно
Franc de port

(Кому Destinataire) Fam. Johann Schni...
Deutschland – ...
Куда (Adresse) Hamburg-Horn Dun...weg...
(страна, город, улица, № дома, округ, с...)

Отправитель (Expéditeur)
Фамилия и имя военнопленного Karl-Heinz Schnibbe
Nom du prisonnier de guerre
U. d. S. S. R.

Почтовый адрес военнопленного
Adresse du prisonnier de guerre Lager 7234

16-я тип. Зак. 365

Front and back sides of a postcard from Russia (an infrequently permitted privilege). Translation on opposite page.

Text of Postcard from Russia—English Translation

December 12, 1948

My dear parents and brother and sister,

How often will I yet write to you? I would never have
believed that I'd still have to be here, but over and over
I've been mistaken. Now again I'm hoping that this will be
the last time I'll write to you. Christmas will soon be here.
How I'd love to be in the circle of my loved ones, whom
I've missed and done without for so long; but fate is
terribly hard, it doesn't inquire about the wishes or the
needs of human beings. It must be this way, or things
would not be as they are. Yet I do not want to give up. I
want to continue to endure, because someday Spring will
come, and then there will be happiness without end. How
are you all otherwise? I hope you're all still well. I'm also
well. I send you all my most heart-felt greetings.

Always thinking of you,

your son and brother Karl-Heinz

was thoroughly innocent and pure. Though her German was
excellent, when the German POWs said something off-color
to her—and I'm afraid our group was not above that, on the
whole—she simply didn't understand the allusion. Even
when someone spelled it out more plainly, she blushed and
was very uncomfortable.

On one of these rail trips into Kuybyshev I had a very
close call. Normally I got along very well on Russian trains;
my Russian was quite good by this time, and I was friendly

to people. When someone came into the compartment, I offered him my seat. The Russians were always surprised to learn that I was a *nemetski*, a German. They immediately started talking to me then.

But once there was an officer in a train compartment who thought my Russian a little too good. "You're no German, you're Vlasov!" The Vlasov army, as I've said, was comprised of Russians who had been willing to fight on the side of Hitler. This officer had fought against the Germans. And he was in a sour mood because he'd been drinking heavily. He pulled out his pistol and said he was going to kill me.

"Why?" I asked. "Why? I am a German!"

"No, no, you're Vlasov!"

I did look like a Russian. My head was shaved, and I was suntanned a deep brown. I wore Russian clothes by then. I was saved when Tamara came into the compartment and said, "Hands off!"

On one of our trips for medical supplies to Kuybyshev we had to wait at some small town for a connection. We were there quite a few hours, so people made themselves comfortable in the dingy little waiting room, sitting or lying on the floor. People just talked, ate, slept, or smoked *makhorka*. When they found out I was a German, they all came over to me—a German POW was like the eighth wonder of the world—and offered me whatever they had: an onion, a tomato, a few sunflower seeds. The women all had their colorful scarves and the children were all barefoot. There was no hatred, just curiosity and friendship.

In another corner of the waiting room there sat an old beggar, a very elderly man with a long, white beard. His little bundle of belongings lay by him. Many of the travellers gave him something to eat as well, and they even gave him a few coins or some *makhorka*. After receiving each gift, the old man crossed himself in the Russian Orthodox manner and gave each person a blessing. They treated him with the same respect they gave to a patriarch. An old *babushka* near me said that he was totally blind.

After a while he took an old, scratched balalaika out of his pack and started to play. At first it was just a few melodic chords, but then suddenly he began to play Russian folk tunes with such energy and beauty as I have seldom heard in my life. I never would have believed that these old, crooked hands could produce such magical sounds on a battered balalaika. Everyone in the room was touched. I was moved to tears. I felt a kinship and a love toward everyone in the room. I remember thinking that the Nazis had called these people subhumans. What irony! These simple Russian people had greatly strengthened my faith in the goodness of mankind and in the grand harmony of the universe. I'll never forget their peasants' faces and the music of the blind balalaika player.

After four years, despite the efforts of Tanya and Dr. Wille, I had declined almost to nothing. I weighed, as I've said, about forty-nine kilos. My legs were like two sticks with a ball in the middle for a knee. Sometimes we prisoners would look at each other and then just start laughing: "Look at you!" I began suffering from night blindness. As soon as the sun went down I couldn't see anything but red rings. Dr. Wille said, "Well, it's not good, but it's not anything to worry about. I think it's reversible if it doesn't go on too long. It's just a vitamin deficiency."

I knew we weren't getting vitamins enough, because one of our camp commanders had apparently sold some of our supplies on the black market and had substituted stinging nettle for it. Since nettle supposedly was rich in vitamins, we began calling him the vitamin king. Dr. Wille had saved a little bit of cod-liver oil, and to prove his point he gave me about a half-teaspoon of it. Immediately thereafter I was able to see again at night for about a week.

When I first got up in the morning I could manage all right, but then about three hours later I was finished. I simply couldn't move. My buttocks were completely gone, so in April of 1949 the medical commission finally told me I could go home. Every day for four years we'd heard *"skoro domoi"* ("You're going home soon") and I'd learned not to get my hopes up, but this time it was true. Georg Wille came to see me and wish me well. He was very happy that I was going home. "I'll see you soon!"

10

Going
Home

About three hundred men from our camp were released at the same time. We walked through the camp gate,
where Tanya met me. She held my hands and with tears in
her eyes she said, "We won't see each other again on this
earth. I'll see you again in heaven."

I was so sick and yet so excited to go home that I could
only mumble, "Good-bye . . . and thanks."

The Volga was still frozen over, even though it was
April, and we were loaded onto trucks and driven on the ice
to the train line. The Volga and the other rivers were the
superhighways when they were frozen. The ice creaked and
there was a film of water on top of it already, but we made it
somehow. The train cars had the usual V-shaped urinal and a
little pot-bellied stove, though there was very little firewood, and it was soon gone, leaving us to sit in the cold. But
we were going home!

A gray column of returning prisoners of war crosses the no-man's-land into freedom. (From a contemporary newspaper.)

We had fewer delays than in 1945, and we reached
Brest-Litovsk and changed to the European gauge. There we
had one last "lice inspection," where we had to lift our arms
and a Russian looked for that little blood type that was tat-
tooed on SS soldiers on the lower part of the bicep near the
armpit. They wanted to make sure no SS were released with
us. If you had a scar there you were in trouble, too, since
they assumed you were an SS man who'd had his tattoo removed. I was surprised that they actually found a few in our
group, after all those years!

Through Poland, for reasons of national security, as we
were told, the doors on our car were nailed shut. When we
got to East Germany, they opened them again. It was getting
warmer already — it was early May by this time — and we sat
in the open doors with our feet hanging down, looking at
the countryside go by. As we passed by, women held up
signs with their sons', husbands', and brothers' names on
them. "Do you know him?" they asked. "Do you have some
bread?" They were hungry, too.

We got to Erfurt, the flower city, where we stayed for
two days in a school, and then we reached Frankfurt on the
Oder, where we received fifty marks each as mustering-out
money. They had a commissary there which sold a hard roll
for fifteen marks, a beer for forty-five, and so forth. Consequently, all the money they gave us stayed right there in
Frankfurt.

In my weakened condition I had picked up an infection
in my left arm. I think a sliver from the boxcars had gotten
in and become infected. I went to see the doctor at Frankfurt
and he told me, "If you can stick it out two or three more
days, have it looked at in the West. If we do it here, we'd
have to keep you here, and heaven knows when you'd get
sent over." Those POWs whose homes were in East
Germany were separated from the rest of us at this big camp

in Frankfurt. They went one way and we went on to the West. The doctor was afraid I might get into the wrong group.

From Frankfurt on the Oder I went to the border crossing at Helmstedt. The Russians delivered us to the border; then there was a two-hundred-yard no-man's-land, with the British waiting for us on the other side. We crossed over as if we were in a dream. We were incredibly happy and excited. The Red Cross gave us hot chocolate and pastry, then we all had to file through a barrack full of the pictures of men who were missing in action. We were supposed to identify any who might still be in Russian camps. Some of our group did see a few who were still there, though I didn't recognize any of them.

From this place we were taken to nearby Goettingen and admitted to a hospital. My arm was immediately lanced, cleaned out, and bandaged. I was put into a room with clean white walls and clean white bedding and I fell asleep. Not long after I was awakened by five or six little girls who had come into my room and were singing a song. I thought the song sounded familiar—and then I realized it was a four-verse song from our LDS hymnbook of that day. It began:

> *O wie wunderbar letzthin ich traeumte,*
> *Noch jetzt es im Ohre mir klingt.*
> *Weit vom Weltengetrieb, in den Taelern lieb,*
> *Wo das Voeglein sein Schlummerlied singt.*

The English words of this delightful song are:

> Oh, I had such a pretty dream, mamma,
> Such pleasant and beautiful things;
> Of a dear little nest in the meadows of rest,
> Where the birdie her lullaby sings.

A dear little stream full of lilies
Crept over the green mossy stones,
And just where I lay, its thin sparkling spray
Sang sweetly in delicate tones.

And as it flowed on toward the ocean
Through shadows and pretty sunbeams,
Each note grew more deep, and I soon fell
    asleep,
And was off to the Island of Dreams.

I saw there a beautiful angel,
With crown all bespangled with dew.
She touched me and spoke, and I quickly
    awoke,
And found there, dear Mamma, 'twas you.

Needless to say, the text of the song made me wonder
for a moment if I had not, in fact, been dreaming the whole
thing, or whether I had died and gone to heaven. But it was
neither of those. Somehow the members of the little branch
of the Church in Goettingen had found out that I was in their
city, perhaps through one of the missionaries working there,
Siegfried Pruess, a boy from the St. Georg Branch in Hamburg. Though I was still very, very sick and had yet to be
reunited with my family, I felt that I had finally come home
at last.

11

Recovering and Adjusting

The Mormons in Goettingen came to visit me regularly. We sent word to my parents that I had been released and was safe. They knew I was alive because I had been allowed to write postcards beginning in July of 1948, and I wrote each month thereafter until January of 1949. Mother and Father wrote back and said that my mother was going to come to Goettingen to see me. I responded that she should wait for a while. I knew they couldn't have had much money, and I didn't want her to see me in my condition. Besides, I wanted to go there, to see them.

I thought that now I was a free man I could sink my teeth into some real food. But the doctors warned me that in my condition overeating could be fatal. They told me of a POW whose home was on a farm near Goettingen who had received a lot of rich food—ham and butter and the like— from his parents, had eaten it, and had died. I got oatmeal and a boiled egg and a mashed potato. Once in a while I got a really lean piece of veal. But even with this diet, my doctor was afraid I was gaining too fast. I had to be tested for blood pressure and heart rhythm every morning, resting, and then after some exercise. "Well," he said, "you seem to have a healthy constitution. You're coming back very fast."

After a few weeks I was given furlough. This meant I was allowed out of the hospital for four hours each afternoon, but I had to be back by 8:00 P.M. We were called *Spaetheimkehrer*, late returnees, so we got free tickets to opera and movie matinees and to other things in town. I also went out often with the missionaries. I still had my Russian clothes — the quilted jacket and the fur hat — so when I went out on the street, everyone could see that I was an ex-POW. I looked like an *"Ivan."* Some people looked at me as though I came from another planet.

One day I received a letter from my brother Bert saying that he was getting married and asking if I could come and be his *Trauzeuge,* or witness. When I asked the doctor, he said, "Absolutely not. You still have the malarial fever."

I said, "Doctor, I insist."

"Impossible!"

"Then I'll just walk away!"

So he brought in a form for me to sign releasing the hospital from any responsibility. They gave me my one-way ticket to Hamburg and told me I'd have to pay my own fare to return to Goettingen for further treatment after the wedding.

The moment I got on the train, people started to come up to me and say, "Oh, excuse me, my name is So-and-so; do you by any chance know my son? His name is So-and-so. Here's his picture." I felt terribly sorry for these people who'd lost their sons and husbands and brothers, but I was also embarrassed. I sat in the corner of the compartment and pulled the window curtain over my face and pretended to be asleep. But women constantly came up to me: "Have you seen my son?" "Haven't you seen my husband?" "Here's a picture." It was very sad.

Finally the train rolled over the Elbe River and I began to bawl like a little boy. I was finally home, in Hamburg. My parents didn't know I was coming, so no one was there to meet me. But later they told me that Mom had been nervous all that morning. She kept going to the window and looking up the street. Dad would say, "What's the matter with you?"

"I don't know."

"Come on, sit down, relax."

"I can't. I just don't know what's the matter."

Since I had no money at all, I had no way of getting from the central station to Horn, where we lived in our former garden house. It would have been impossible for me to walk that far in my condition. Even the tram took a half-hour. Finally I just decided to get on the streetcar. Soon the conductor came along and asked if there were any riders who didn't have tickets. I didn't say anything, hoping he'd leave me alone, but he saw me and said, "Do you have a ticket?"

"No."

"Where are you going?"

"Dunckersweg, the Bauerberg stop, in Horn."

"Okay; that'll be thirty-five pfennig."

"I don't have thirty-five pfennig."

"Then you'll have to get off at the next stop!"

Meanwhile, a lot of people had overheard our conversation. They jumped up and surrounded the poor conductor. "You stupid idiot," they yelled at him. "Can't you see where this man has been?"

They asked me, "Are you just returning from Russia?"

"Yes."

Then they all thrust money at the man: "Here, you idiot, here's your crummy thirty-five pfennig!" I felt sorry for him, because he'd have been in trouble if his supervisor had caught him letting me ride free, but I was gratified at the way the people responded.

The wedding was a wonderful reunion with my family. They all made a fuss over me, yet treated me like someone who had only been away for a little while, not like a stranger. "How's it going?" "Come on over here and sit down!" There was music and good food. It was a very gratifying, heartwarming experience.

After two days I had to get back to Goettingen. But I didn't have a train ticket. Mom said, "Well, we'll find the money somehow." But just then the other *Trauzeuge*, Jean Wunderlich, overheard us and said, "I'm going right through Goettingen on my way to Frankfurt. I'll drop you off!"

My parents didn't have any money, but they were loaded with food and clothing which had been shipped to Germany by the American Mormons. A third had been sent to the Catholic relief agency, a third to the Protestant one, and a third to the Mormons. Otto Berndt, who had replaced Soellner as the St. Georg Branch president (the latter had moved to the Harburg Branch) had rented an old air raid shelter for a warehouse, which now was full of food and clothing. Since I was going back to Goettingen by car, we filled a big suitcase with canned peaches and pears, intending to share it with the doctors and nurses in Goettingen, who were themselves having trouble finding enough to eat. I threw away my Russian clothes and outfitted myself with a couple of pairs of pants, a sports jacket, several shirts, lots of socks and underwear, and a pair of shoes. This was not just used hand-me-down clothing; it was all first-class, new, American stuff. Overnight I went from looking like a rather shabby *"Ivan"* to looking like a very spiffy *"Ami."*

Jean Wunderlich and I and Hans Dahl, our driver, left for Goettingen in Jean's big DeSoto. American automobiles, of course, were something like the eighth wonder of the world in postwar Germany, so when we rolled up to the hospital, right at noon when lots of people were sitting outside in the sun, we made quite a sensation: "Who's that well-dressed *Ami* in the *Strassenkreuzer* (street-cruiser)? Hey, it's Schnibbe!" I distributed all the food I had brought, and then I went back to bed for another few weeks, trying to get my malaria cleared up.

Finally, on June 3, 1949, I was released from the hospital in Goettingen and I returned home. My parents and my grandfather Luetkemueller were living, as I've said, in our former garden shed, a prefabricated house which was about twelve feet by twelve feet. But in the meantime they had collected bricks, which were abundant in all the rubble, and hauled them home on their wagon. With these they built on a little brick addition.

Food was still being rationed, but since Dad was sometimes working two eight-hour shifts a day as an overhead crane operator at the port and I was a returned POW, both he and I were eligible for the "heavy laborer" category of food ration coupons. These, together with the food and clothing shipments from America, meant that we got along relatively well in this difficult period.

In addition, I discovered when I went downtown to the office which issued food coupons that the postwar German government had placed my name on a list of those persecuted by the Nazis, and that I was entitled to reparations payments. I was invited by the *Vereinigung der Verfolgten des Nazi Regimes,* the association of those persecuted by the Nazi regime, to come to their headquarters.

The *VVN* people welcomed me warmly and sincerely; there was nothing phoney or unctuous about them. They presented me with a check for two thousand Deutschmarks and sent me to a warehouse, where I was given a suit of clothes and an overcoat. Altogether, in semi-annual installments, I received ten thousand DM in reparations. With this money I was later able to emigrate to the United States.

The *VVN* people told me they'd written to the Soviet government as early as 1947 in an attempt to free those antifascists who, like me, were being held in Russian camps. In my case it hadn't helped, of course, but I was happy to find out that someone had been trying.

The *VVN* offered to pay for a stay in a sanatorium if I wished to go there to recuperate, but I didn't want to leave home again. I also declined an invitation to take part in a convention of the *VVN* in East Berlin. I was not happy about their Communist connections; besides, I felt a bit uncomfortable about all the fuss people were making over me. I just wanted to get my health and my life back to normal again.

I must have been eager to get back to where the nightmare had started, because I immediately went to see Johannes Ehlers, my old boss at the painting firm of F. Georg Suse. His wife met me at the door and told me he was dead, but she offered me a job on the spot. "Start tomorrow," she said. However, my doctors had told me not to start working too soon—for six months, to be exact. I was still very emaciated. With the reparations money I had enough to live on and help my parents, and I felt that I ought to take the doctors' advice. So I reluctantly decided to rest for a while, but I promised her I'd be back.

And gradually I got better. Physically, that is. Psychologically, I had a slower adjustment. The medical people cared for my body and the *VVN* provided for my worldly needs, but no one really inquired about the state of my soul. Yet I had some serious problems. I'd wake up at night, bathed in cold sweat, reliving over and over again my experiences in the camps. Even when I was awake I was adrift. I didn't feel that I belonged anywhere. I felt restless. I had grown used to being told what to do—I had even gotten used to the yells and the kicks—but now here I was, completely on my own. If anything, people were too deferential to the poor, unfortunate POW.

I had gone into that series of prisons as an adolescent. Because I had devoted almost all my energy for seven years to my own survival, without really experiencing any personal development in the meantime, I now emerged from the prisons a selfish—albeit older—adolescent, with social skills that were almost completely stunted or inappropriate to normal society. I was self-centered, unable to relate to others and their problems or points of view. And I was lewd, crude, and rude. For a time I was sure that my soul had been permanently scarred—that I had been reduced by my experiences to the very level of a beast. I lived in fear of hurting someone around me, especially my family.

My parents sensed that there was something wrong. When I'd sit and stare into space my mother would say, "Karl-Heinz!" and I wouldn't hear her. Then Dad would ask Mom, "What's the matter with the boy? What's wrong?"

Mom always said, "Just leave him alone." Mom understood my heart; she knew how torn it was, that I was trying hard, but that I was still far away sometimes, still in Russia, still in the camps, still with Helmuth at the trial. Some days I'd just get on a streetcar and ride all day with no destination. I visited an aunt once who had invited me to dinner, and then I just got up and walked out. I wandered around until midnight and then I went home.

Then one day, just before Christmas in 1949, Mother and I went together to one of the free organ concerts which were always held in the major churches on Saturdays. During the concert I began to cry. People came up to us and asked, "What's the matter? Are you sick? Can we help you?"

And Mom said, "Leave him alone, let him cry. That'll wash it all out." I got up and left the church and paced around outside. I cried for over two hours. In the end the music and the tears had purged and washed my soul, as mother had said, and I now felt that there was hope. My soul was not permanently scarred after all. I was still a human being.

To this day music is my salvation. I never miss the symphony. I love the great romantics, especially the melancholy Russians, Dvorak's *New World*, Grieg, and some Wagner, such as the Pilgrim's Chorus from *Tannhauser*, and *Lohengrin* and *Parsifal* and the *Ring*.

I worked hard to rid myself of my profanity, which seemed to me an audible reminder of the past, and step by step I improved. "The good Lord gave us two ears, one to let it in and one to let it out," I reminded myself from then on whenever I heard profanity—which was not uncommon, especially after I went back to work.

In some ways the Church was helpful in my fight for readjustment, and in some ways it was not. My branch president, Otto Berndt, whom I dearly love and respect, felt that one ought to go down on one's knees and talk to God about one's problems, not to some other mortal. Perhaps he is right, ultimately, but I think I could also have used wise human counsel and a listening human ear. The Church members did help me by treating me like an old friend and allowing me to mingle with them like a normal person. Most of them ignored the obvious fact that I still smoked, and they were most gracious.

My friend Rudi was there in our branch. He'd been liberated from Hahnoefersand by the British in 1945 and had been given a pistol and told to guard his former guards, who were now behind bars in his cell! He had promised the Lord that he'd serve a mission if he survived, so he went as soon as he was able. Now he was back from his mission and he welcomed me with open arms.

Except for Rudi, no one in our branch ever mentioned Helmuth and our ordeal. Even though I was often bursting to talk about it, no one ever asked me to tell them about my experiences. They all seemed to want to repress it, to forget about the past. It's as if there was a conspiracy of silence. Of course, many of the members were new; they were refugees from the eastern provinces or they had joined the Church after our arrest.

Still, we were like one big happy family, and everyone was friendly to me. One night my brother took me to a dance at the Harburg Branch. I didn't want to go at first, but he persuaded me. Naturally Arnold Soellner was there—he was the branch president—but we got along fine. He was very friendly.

I began going to other dances then. Even though I may have had some complexes, I was also hungry for life. I bought expensive clothes for myself and tried to impress the girls, because I felt so insecure around them. I even began to date a few, some members and some nonmembers, with whom I felt a little more comfortable, since I still had my smoking habit.

I began to visit some old acquaintances. In addition to Rudi and Otto Berndt, Jr., and my brother and sister, whom I visited regularly, I went to see our old neighbor, the SA man Otto Schulz. He got tears in his eyes when he saw me. "You know," he said, "when you got arrested I was ready to go to the Gestapo and tell them you'd shown me a leaflet and that you didn't mean any harm."

"You dumb fool," I said. "If you'd done that they'd have hanged you the next minute!"

During the denazification process, Schulz had lost his job as an official with the post office. They had demoted him to letter carrier, and he'd lost his pension and everything. I'd have liked to go downtown and put in a good word for him, but by then it was too late. He had been a "party partaker," in Helmuth's words, and now it had caught up with him. But at least he was honest—not like those who were Nazis and then, suddenly, in 1945 had been Social Democrats and secret resistance fighters all their lives!

Eventually, near the end of 1949, I went back to work. I was readjusting well enough, I thought, that I could now start to contemplate marriage. I'd met a willing young lady, an LDS girl, who liked me and who had motherly instincts and who said, "Oh, you poor guy!" I, in turn, needed someone to cling to. We had enough money and I had a good job, so what could make more sense than to tie the knot? But the moment we were married, the instant I said "I do," I knew I'd made a serious mistake. She wanted a normal husband and I was anything but normal yet. All my selfish survival skills got in my way. All my prison instincts to watch out for "number one" caused problems in my marriage. (My advice to people who've been in prison camps is to wait at least ten years before getting married!)

And I felt trapped. In some ways it was like being in prison again. I simply was not mature enough to care for anyone else besides myself. I was simply overwhelmed by someone who loved me. I didn't know how to handle that. And yet I prolonged the agony because I hated to admit to myself or to others that I'd made such a foolish mistake. Divorce is not taken lightly in our culture, and I didn't want to be a disgrace to my family. So the years went by, with each of us living more or less separate lives. Every day I'd "go home" to see my mother, who was still the only one who understood her unhappy old adolescent son.

12

New Country,
New Life

In the spring of 1951, my brother Bert emigrated to the United States. His brother-in-law had preceded him, writing back enthusiastic letters about what a wonderful place America was. Everybody had a house and at least two cars! Latter-day Saints in Germany knew that they could do more good for the Church by staying there, but the allure of worldly goods was just too strong, in most cases. During these lean, postwar years, we had a farewell almost every Sunday in the branch for some family or other who were emigrating. So Bert gave up his very good, very promising job as an employment agent for movie and theatre actors, left the country just before the "economic miracle" made Germany wealthy, and came to the United States, where he worked at a menial job in a soda bottling factory for minimum wage.

But we knew none of this, of course, and my wife's mother was in America as well, so in January of 1952 we

Karl-Heinz and Rennly Charlesworth gold-leafing in Symphony Hall, Salt Lake City.

decided to give it a try. We had our tickets and enough reparations money to buy return trips if we didn't like it, and I told myself it was an adventure, an extended trip which I could cut short and return home from at any time.

Our voyage on the SS *America* lasted five days. We docked in New York and went through immigration proceedings in just a few minutes. Because I had a trade and because I was a victim of Nazi persecution, I had gotten a visa with no problems. "Were you a Nazi?" the form inquired. "No, I was in a concentration camp," I wrote. We had a sponsor, Elwood Barker, who had been a missionary in Germany in 1924 and had blessed me as a baby. We spent three weeks on Long Island with my aunt—my father's cousin, actually—and then we took a train to Salt Lake City. During the three days and two nights on the train, I was constantly reminded of my travels in Russia. Both countries are so big!

I didn't worry much about learning English. I'd learned Russian, and I was confident that I'd do all right with English as well. I was not inhibited; I simply started jabbering and hoped that people would correct me.

I got a job right away with a painting and decorating contractor named Alfred A. Lippold, a German who had emigrated from Saxony in the thirties. He was one of the best around. He did all the fancy decorating work on older LDS chapels and on the temples. In America I have had the privilege of gold leafing several Angel Moroni statues for the spires of Mormon temples, and I did the gold work in the new Symphony Hall in Salt Lake City and in many other places—plus striping, stenciling, and wallpapering, and fine finishing of every kind.

I soon learned what kind of paints and other materials there were here in the United States; I was generally pleased at the high quality. We didn't have flat enamel paint in Germany, for example; we had to use glossy enamel and then rub the gloss out with pumice. It was beautiful, and so slick a fly couldn't stand up on it, but it took a lot of hard work. I soon learned that in the United States the lowest bid gets the job, and I picked up the expression, "Well, you get what you pay for."

We found an apartment in the Avenues area of Salt Lake City, a cute little furnished place. At first I went to the German-speaking ward, and then I said to myself: "Wait a minute; what am I doing here? I've got to learn English!" And so I went to the Third Ward, an English-speaking ward, and got involved right away. I still went to the monthly German meetings in the Assembly Hall and I sang with the German choir, which I enjoyed very much. I eventually began playing with a German repertory company, as well, but I was going to try to be an American!

My bishop wanted me to be ordained an elder, but first I needed to quit smoking. I was tired of sneaking around anyway, hiding ashtrays whenever the doorbell rang, keeping a spray can of room deodorant and a pocketful of mints handy. My mother-in-law had even asked me to take my jacket out of her closet because it smelled so bad, so I struggled with the habit and eventually I beat it.

It's not that I hid away in the meantime. I went to church regularly and I paid my tithing. "Sin with honor!" I said. "The sick, the smokers, need the Church as much as the nonsmokers!" To their great credit, no one ever moved away from me on a pew and no one ever made an unkind remark about the smell, and eventually I overcame the habit. I had begun to smoke in the camps to kill the hunger pangs, and now one more relic from my past was gone, thank goodness.

Even as I became more and more committed to the Church, my wife became less and less interested in it, so I always went alone. Eventually the inevitable happened and we were divorced. I take the responsibility for our problems.

I met and married her before I was completely healed. I simply was not the same person then and after ten years. I was not ready yet for marriage. Unfortunately, she really belonged to my old self, to my past, and the whole marriage seems like a bad dream, a continuation of my life in the camps. I am now remarried to a wonderful woman, and we are confident of success in our mutual efforts to make a happy life together.

One of the great appeals of America to Germans in those days was the automobile. We all secretly wanted a car. I bought a Chevy not long after I arrived here, and I washed and polished it almost every day. It had big, wide whitewall tires and they were always gleaming. Before it was even paid for I got a new one.

After five years I was eligible to become naturalized, and exactly five years to the day I became a citizen. My parents and my sister had joined us in the meantime. I enjoyed it in the United States, and I had given up any thought of moving back to Germany. I also felt that I ought to participate in our democracy, to remove people where I felt they shouldn't be in power and work to install those who should. I had suffered enough under the totalitarianisms of this century so that the democratic process was especially precious to me.

I got involved in the leadership of the painters' union for the same reasons. I simply don't think one ought to turn over one's fate to a small minority who make secret deals in back rooms. I had seen what can happen if the people are not vigilant. Even though it is not always convenient or pleasant, I try very hard to be informed and to exercise my voting franchise and my other civic responsibilities.

One issue which immediately struck me upon my arrival in the United States was that of the civil rights of racial minorities, especially blacks. There were not many blacks in

Salt Lake City. The only blacks I knew were wonderful people. But I saw the newspapers and I saw how they were being treated as a whole throughout the nation. "Uh, oh," I said to myself, "that sounds so familiar!" It reminded me so strongly of the treatment of Jews, the "subhumans" in Germany after 1933. I happened to be very sensitive to such discrimination. I followed and supported the civil rights movements very carefully, and when President Spencer W. Kimball's revelation on blacks and the priesthood came in 1978, I was overjoyed. I was also thrilled to see that the vast majority of Latter-day Saints were as happy as I was, that they wholeheartedly accepted it.

Even though we've been tempted and made serious mistakes, in the long run this country has refused to act in a totalitarian way, like a new Hitler Germany. We, the people, have struggled to end racial discrimination, to end the war in Vietnam, to peacefully divest ourselves of a corrupt president, and to take other important strides away from repression and toward equality and justice and peace. I'm proud to be able to live here and participate in the struggle.

In 1962, ten years after I emigrated, I returned for a visit to Hamburg. I felt as if I'd been away only a month or so. But after about three weeks I grew homesick for the United States. Germany is a wonderful country, with rich democratic traditions now, and my love for Hamburg is still very strong, but friends move away and things change. I'm occasionally homesick for Germany, even now, perhaps even more, the older I become. I've been back for visits on seven occasions, but my home is here now and I love it.

Rudi Wobbe and his wife Herta came to the United States some time after I did. He's had his worries, of course, and I've had mine, but we have remained good friends to this day. Rudi is a machinist, a foreman in a machine shop here. He seems to like his work and he's successful at it. Otto

Berndt Senior and Junior are here as well. So are Helmuth's half brothers.

Some other German immigrants have not done as well. Frankly, I think it is a simple function of age: Those who were younger than, say, forty when they came to the United States, got along all right on the whole, especially if they did not go into a linguistic ghetto and neglect learning English. Older Germans had more problems, by and large. They often had to accept menial jobs like that of janitor, either because they had no trade or the language barrier kept them from working in their trade. That's what happened to my brother. I was fortunate to be able to step right into a profession that I loved and keep right on working.

Some immigrants were bothered by the fact that the people in Utah had faults. They had come to Zion, as it were, and they subconsciously expected everything to be perfect. When it was not, they were deeply disappointed. In addition, most of them had been very, very active and important members of their relatively small German branches. Now they were lost in large Utah wards, and they felt lucky if someone asked them to say the closing prayer in church meetings.

Others were never quite able to make the social and cultural adjustments necessary to get along here. Some made faux pas like saying, "Now, in Germany we don't have crooked ceilings like that. . . . In Germany this is much better and in Germany that is done differently." The inevitable response to such nostalgia was: "Why don't you go back there if you like it so much?!"

Others never quite learned that Americans are likely to be more tactful and less blunt than Germans. When someone would say, "Oh, how nice to see you. Come visit me sometime," the Germans often did. When someone asked a German's opinion about, say, a new painting or rug, the German, thinking that an opinion was really wanted, often gave a brutally honest one, which was not always complimentary.

I made my share of cultural mistakes here too. I stepped on a lot of people's toes. But I eventually learned to appreciate Americans for their freer spirits, for not being so harsh and so judgmental. Rather than dismissing them as wishy-washy, which was normal for Germans to do, I learned to like the feeling that I was welcome in every house, and that people were friendly and warm. Perhaps my background helped me to adjust. I had learned to duck and to roll with the punches, so to speak, and I knew I was a survivor, that I could adjust to anything. That gave me the confidence I needed to keep on trying to adapt.

All in all, in the long term all my suffering, all my trying experiences in Nazi Germany and in Soviet Russia and afterwards, have been for my own good and have stood me in good stead. As bad as my experiences were in the short term, as I think back on them now I feel that I am better for having undergone them. They not only taught me that I could adapt to anything, but they also taught me to be more understanding of people and their condition and situation and point of view. They taught me to appreciate the gift of life, every minute of it, and to live it to the fullest.

Along the way I acquired a deep appreciation for freedom and a sense of the need we have to defend it. Living in the United States has naturally enhanced these concepts and feelings. I perceive the seeds of these convictions as I look back on my childhood and youth under parental influence.

And I perceive in my friend Helmuth Huebener, under whose influence I also came during those long-past years, an understanding and love of freedom well beyond the norm for one so young. To him this book is gratefully dedicated.